OLD SHANKLIN
SPA RESORT OF THE NOBILITY

ARTHUR W. J. G. ORD-HUME

The paddle steamer *Southsea*, launched in May of 1930, pays a visit to Shanklin Pier just after the restoration of the Pierhead jetties. The shallow-gabled building on the very end of the Pier bears a notice reading 'Shanklin's Pleasure Pier' while a small noticeboard advertises the Chine in the hope that it may inspire those disembarking to seek out its attractions. Built at Govan, *Southsea* was requisitioned by the Navy for war service and was credited with shooting down an enemy aircraft. On February 16th, 1941, she struck a mine and was lost with the lives of two officers and five ratings.

Stenlake Publishing Ltd.

© 2022 Arthur W. J. G. Ord-Hume
First Published in the United Kingdom, 2022
Stenlake Publishing Limited
54-58 Mill Square, Catrine, KA5 6RD

01290 551122
www.stenlake.co.uk

ISBN 978-1-84033-942-0

P2D Books, 1 Newlands Rd, Westoning, Bedford MK45 5LD

The right of Arthur W. J. G. Ord-Hume as author of this work has been asserted by him in accordance with the Copyright, Designs and Patent Act, 1993.

All rights reserved. No part of this publication may be reproduced, stored in a retrieval system, or transmitted in any form or by any means, electronic, mechanical, photocopying, recording or otherwise, without the prior permission of Stenlake Publishing Limited.

British Library Cataloguing in Publication Data:
A catalogue record for this book is available from the British Library.

> All who have seen leafy Shanklin speak tenderly of it. Who can avoid, who need avoid speaking gently of the sweet hanging curtains of green that clothe this lovely spot. It is so human, if we may be allowed the word. Blackgang is ghastly in its barrenness and its remorseless divorce from vegetation. Shanklin is sweet with shadow, leafy twitterings, the murmur of a prattling streamlet, and the fall of a tiny waterfall. Nay, the very presence of the little perched-up friendly inn. The woman with her baskets of pebble jewellery, which without a blush she tells you is all made on the Isle from stones found on the beach, the gates, the seats, the rustic bridge, - all help to produce a sense of comfort, and give humanity to the scene.
>
> from the article on Shanklin contained in *The Isle of Wight* by J Redding Ware published by Provost & Co, London, 1869

Acknowledgements

In compiling this pictorial history of Shanklin I acknowledge the work of those many others who have gone before me. First and foremost I have to thank my parents who introduced me to the place when I was a small boy in the 1930s. They had discovered Shanklin the way most 'overners' do – as mere holidaymakers. That I should end up living there when I left the Royal Air Force and become closely involved in both Shanklin and Island affairs for a good quarter-century from the 1950s onwards was my good fortune.

I am grateful to all those photographers who took their pictures of Shanklin way back in the early days of photography. I acknowledge with equal gratitude the picture postcard makers who spent their time unwittingly recording local history for posterity through the commercial aspirations of their lenses.

Head and shoulders above them stand the Nigh family, initially of Ventnor, then of Shanklin – and still going strong. They were picture postcard publishers and took many thousands of glass plates of Shanklin and elsewhere through their lenses. Thankfully in their new offices today these pictures are preserved in the hands of Terry Nigh and his younger successors.

The work of the Shanklin & District History Society plays an important part in my story for members of this organisation, in particular Terry Nigh and Andrew Asher, have assisted me over the years.

A word about my illustrations. Some come from picture postcards but a significant majority are from actual photographs including many from fragile early albumen prints which after more than one and a half centuries are often frail, torn and stained. A minimum amount of reconstructive retouching has been carried out where necessary. There are also many photographs that I have taken over the years from the 1930s (with a 116-size Box Brownie) to the post-war years with 35mm and medium-format cameras.

The late Desmond Norman, founder-director of Bembridge-based aircraft manufacturers Britten-Norman Ltd was once interviewed on a BBC TV programme broadcast from a local Island venue. One of the questions his interviewer posed was 'how long does it take a person from the mainland to be accepted as an Islander' to which Desmond responded with his usual dry humour 'About seven generations!' While that verges on the uncharitable, there is a vaguely sardonic element in it. Islanders are rather special people. They gaze northwards and talk of the big island over the water…

Preface

I have had a soft spot for Shanklin for a long, long while. It was one of the places that topped the holiday destinations of my parents and we were regular visitors. The best hotel was The Royal Spa on the Esplanade, so we always stayed there. Shanklin had every attraction that a good Georgian might seek – bowls, tennis, golf, archery, shooting… And behind the railway station and down a lane was another attraction – Shanklin's own aerodrome where I was introduced to that other love of my life – flying.

My formative years were spent exploring this place. I hesitate to call it a village, although it is proud of its Old Village, and I falter at referring to it as a town, for that implies traffic, noise and the opposite of relaxation. I also demur to use the popular terminology of the past era where Shanklin is referred to as 'a sleepy village settlement' which, I consider, both patronising and insulting besides being quite wrong. I think that the word 'place' serves it well, for you can't pick fault with a non-critical term. Yes, OK. I am being pedantic. I am sorry.

When, after the war, I got the chance of a job on the Island, initially as assistant chief designer for a newly-formed firm of aircraft designers and manufacturers, I was in my element. Naturally I chose Shanklin as my home and quickly integrated with the community, finally contributing as residents' representative on the local council.

From here I explored the Island and each time concluded that Shanklin was by far the best place. Sadly it is not a judgement I would agree with today as things have rather gone downhill. No, Shanklin today is the venue for those who fall short of the stimulus that takes youth to the far corners of the world on a modern-day version of the Victorians' 'Grand Tour'. Today people prefer to talk of the Bahamas, Sri Lanka, Africa and Australia, hopefully gaining kudos for speaking of far-flung attractions as if they know them ever so well. Shanklin's not in that league.

Once it was different. The Isle of Wight represented excitement and Sandown Bay sunshine, sand, warmth and comfort. Talking about Shanklin elevated you to the class of person that hobnobbed with the aristocracy. Shanklin was where you met fellow people of class; the sort of people you would like to be associated with. If it was good enough for Keats, then it was most certainly good enough for you!

To participate in the regular sight-seeing tours led by those smartly-turned-out grooms at Daish's that steered a coach-load of smartly-turned-out visitors around the Island by impeccably kempt horses put one in that van of people that wanted to be seen with others of the same ilk. And to stay at Hollier's meant that you were no ordinary tourist taking the air on a budget. After all, Elgar honeymooned there.

Those rich days are in the distant past. As the world has advanced in every way, air travel has made access to foreign places easy and affordable. We choose to ignore those resultant high bands of disturbed and polluted air that airliners produce and which affect our weather and foster global warming. Vast cruise liners emulate floating cities as they criss-cross the oceans. Their underwater sounds disorientate fish and other marine life and they leave trails of non-biodegradable waste behind them.

The price of progress has altered the balance of our lives and destroyed forever our innate sense of wonder. It takes ever-more spectacular things to satisfy us. Simple pleasures have become more involved and something as inconsequential as a peaceful holiday resort scores a very low mark on the 'to do' list.

Once our Island had Royal patronage. Our then Queen lived at Osborne. The Victorian age was also rich in attracting foreign nobility and royalty. Shanklin was well-loved by the many members of the German and French aristocracy. Not without good reason did Shanklin's council ensure that the annual guidebook was not only well-produced and copiously illustrated, but was published with a fulsome summary in the German and French languages. And the owner of The Royal Spa Hotel had a flag-pole and made a habit of hoisting the standard of the top foreign visitor staying at his establishment.

A picture book about Shanklin! My problem is that I have too many illustrations – photographs, picture post-cards and engravings. I have tried to give you a good representative selection. Some are very old and of poor quality but, if they are important, they are included since I am sure you would rather see a bad picture of a rare event rather than not at all. The popularity of my earlier book, *The Royal Spa: A History of Shanklin Esplanade*, convinced me that there was a need for the present work. Views are repeated where they show significant changes, the Old Village being one example.

A word of caution on dates. Some postcards were in circulation for a long while so you cannot always date a view by its postmark. Other pictures were of short-lived events and these were the contemporary version of the 'local paper' type of picture coverage.

To help you date your own images, then, I have added a time-line. This tells you when notable things happened like when the Lift was built, the Pier, the Jubilee Clock (not, note, in the Jubilee year!) and so on. At the very least it will enable you to date picture postcard illustrations more reliably: postmarks conceal the fact that sometimes a card might be in circulation for a year or more.

Which brings me to picture captions. Many of these are inordinately long and for this I am sorry but if a story is worth telling it is worth telling *in extensis*. I hope you agree with me here. If not, let me apologise in advance. I have also included some illustrations of retail shops that record an enterprising diversity of items for hire or sale.

Shanklin

The name 'Shanklin' is of some considerable antiquity. It is said to have originated in the Early Middle Ages, specifically by the Anglo-Saxons which suggests between the years from 410 to 1066. People of that time called the area 'Scenc-hlinc' or 'cup in the rising ground' – a sort of deep, scooped-out hollow.

For many hundreds of years Shanklin was a mere scattering of insignificant farmers and fishermen. Its antiquity did, though, earn it a mention in the Domesday Book – that survey of England and Wales completed in the year 1086 by order of William the Conqueror. Even so, despite being one of the Island's oldest settlements, it was to remain largely unknown to the outside world until some nine hundred years later.

Indeed, in the past, Shanklin was so small and insignificant that, along with equally tiny Sandown, it came under the jurisdiction of Brading. This inspired an early guidebook (*Black's Picturesque Guide to the Isle of Wight*) to say 'It is 4 miles from Shanklin to Brading, and is certainly now the most uninteresting 4 miles in the Isle of Wight. The rage for building, and for building in its worst phases, has done its best to spoil what was once a charming four miles' walk.

While it was probably the infamous essayist and radicalist John Wilkes (1725-1797) that put Sandown on the map (he built a small house there adding what Winter (*The Enchanted Isle*) described as 'a touch of colour and eccentricity' to the place), Shanklin was merely associated with agriculture and fishing until the middle of the 19th century. It was also not a minor player in the practice of smuggling, but that's another subject altogether.

The person who appears to have elevated the area from the inauspicious to the notable was none other than the poet Keats.

John Keats (1795—1821) lived a distressingly short life yet packed into it much in the way of achievements. He lived in Shanklin between 1817 and 1819 staying in the Old Village at what was then known as Eglantine Cottage in Pomona Road. This was one of only two lodging houses in the village. Keats wrote warmly of the place and his words alerted the world at large that here was a spot worth visiting. It is known that he penned parts of *On the Sea* and *Hyperion* while he was living at this address.

Although he died in distant Rome two years later at the age of only 25, his brief life left an indelible mark on what others chose to describe as 'one of the prettiest villages in the Isle of Wight'. Others, probably a little less charitable, referred to it as 'a remote and sleepy little village'.

Jane Austen also came to Shanklin. Recording the event in June 8th, 1813, she said: 'We hired a sociable & drove around the Eastern and Southern coasts of the Island – saw the Priory a sweet place - Shanklin Chine, lovely!'

Shanklin seems to have attracted interesting people throughout the years for none other than the naturalist, geologist and biologist Charles Darwin (1809-1882) stayed at Norfolk House, one of the few houses on the Esplanade before it was much more than a few cottages and a sea wall. It was here that he and his wife sojourned in 1858; he had married his cousin Emma in 1838. He wrote of his stay: 'we think this the nicest sea-side place which we have ever seen, and we like Shanklin better than other sea-side spots on the south coast of the Island.' It is possible that he wrote some of his masterful book *Origin of Species* in this building.

The coming of the Romantic Age heralded a new appreciation of beautiful scenery and bucolic surroundings. Shanklin ticked all the right boxes and what today we call its picturesque Old Village with its thatched cottages and peaceful Chine began to attract visitors.

The American poet Henry Wadsworth Longfellow (1807-1882) stayed at Hollier's Hotel in 1868. He wrote of the place: 'This is one of the quietest and loveliest places in the kingdom' and left charming words that are now inscribed upon a small shield above a drinking-fountain outside the hotel at the entrance to the Chine:

> O traveller stay thy weary feet
> > Drink of this fountain, pure and sweet
> It flows for rich and poor the same
> > Then go thy way, remembering still
> The wayside well beneath the hill,
> > The cup of water in His name.

It was the discovery of strong local springs of chalybeate water containing allegedly health-giving minerals that revolutionised things and upon which Shanklin was to build its reputation as a Spa town during the late Victorian and Edwardian period. In fact it did more for it spread a new fame far and wide, putting the place on an international map. Shanklin quickly gained a reputation as an exclusive holiday destination amongst the German and Russian Royal Families.

This water which flowed freely from the rocks behind today's Esplanade and also from Small Hope Beach at one end and close to the Chine at the other, brought about a massive change in Shanklin's popularity. Various doctors willingly gave their names to analyses of this liquid and concluded that it was both health-giving and extremely good for body and mind. The benefits of good health to all who drank of it were such that people willingly overlooked its foul taste and smell.

Shanklin could now promote itself as a genuine Spa venue to rival other European destinations. This largely succeeded and, aided by the experience of sea travel, it soon gained a reputation that was high on the bucket list of the aristocracy.

Shanklin, though, had other, lesser springs. In fact, the whole rocky coast was rich in water courses. This on its own was no problem. The real snag was that the land rested on a sloping layer of gault – a type of clay, blue/black in colour, known locally as 'blue slipper'. Following a wet winter, the gault tended to absorb water and this acted as a lubricant between the rocks above and below, whereupon they became prone to sliding. The result was that the ground become mobile as it started to slip away in a series of landslides.

Even so, Adam and Charles Black of Edinburgh, after their scathing comments in earlier editions, remained less than charitable about Shanklin in their 1882 Guide Book. After quoting from the effusive writings of Lord Jeffrey, they add:

> Shanklin has become a tolerable-sized town and there having been no definite plan adopted in laying it out, but every man being left to follow his own devices, the beauty of the place has been sadly marred, The Chine is much visited notwithstanding the charge (3d.) for admission.

One can be certain that Shanklin was on the itinerary of most visitors to the Island and quite early on that the place to which was appended the cod-Latin name Southern Vectis was known to foreigners. A godson of Emperor Napoléon I, Napoléon Joseph Ney, Prince de la Moskowa (1803-1857), was a French soldier and politician who apparently enjoyed visiting the Isle of Wight. While he did not mention Shanklin by name, a visit he made in the summer of 1851 drew the following general remarks:

> Of all parts of England, the Isle of Wight is perhaps the one where one can, with the least fatigue and expense, travel to the most interesting places in the shortest space of time. I have come very often to this charming island, so close to France, so favoured by its location and its climate, and, strangely enough, I have never met a single one of my compatriots there.

Much later on, the author and journalist Stuart Petre Brodie Mais (1885–1975) better known as S P B Mais, said of Shanklin:

> (It) is not only a jewel, but a collection of jewels, and a holiday spent here is an accumulation of countless gem-like moments.'

Small though it was in overall size, Shanklin possessed then as now some interesting and, in several instances, unique attractions, both natural and architectural.

Take, for example, the ancient church of St Blasius on the southern-most outskirts of the town. George Brannon wrote dismissively in his 23rd annual volume *The Pleasure Visitor's Companion to the Tour of the Isle of Wight* (1851);

> The church is an uninteresting object in itself, but forms an agreeable feature in the general landscape: is passed on our road to Bonchurch.

This might be the chink in the great man's armour, for it is altogether accepted as a pleasing and peaceful haven. By far the oldest church in town, its origins go back to the reign of King Stephen which means between 1135 and 1154. Originally a plain rectangular planform, the addition of transepts enlarged the building greatly and created a novel situation whereby the bells in the now-central tower are rung from the middle of the church in full view of the congregation.

St Blasius is famed for another feature which is not actually part of the church but a good hundred yards away – its lychgate. This substantial gateway contains a fully-working and striking clock which displays the time to travellers. The clock and bell were given to the church by the residents of Shanklin as a memorial to the Lord Mayor of Shanklin, Francis White Popham, the last resident Lord of the Manor, on his passing in 1894.

When, on May 8th, 1889, the 29-year-old composer Edward Elgar married one of his pupils, Caroline Alice Roberts, known as Alice, they followed in the footsteps of Keats and Longfellow and spent the first week of their honeymoon at Hollier's Hotel.

At the start of the 20th century, Shanklin had no fewer than two local newspapers. The first was *The Gazette* published from premises opposite Daish's Hotel and owned by Martin Silsbury. Second was *The Isle of Wight Guardian*. This was produced in Regent Street in a building subsequently rebuilt for the F W Woolworth store in 1936. This journal, which first appeared about 1880, was owned and edited by a man named Shaker Rogers who seems to have come from the New Forest. The *Guardian* eventually passed into the hands of the Saunders family, the late George Gordon Saunders being editor/proprietor for a major part of his life. The paper was to amalgamate with the *Gazette* and, in more recent times, the *Isle of Wight Chronicle* at Sandown, after which it was known as *The Isle of Wight Chronicle and Guardian*.

Even so, Shanklin was still considered to be but a small and insignificant place as late as 1884 for in Davenport Adams' *The Isle of Wight* ('especially adapted to the wants of the tourist and excursionist'), while he devotes several pages to it, he does not think it worthy of a separate distinction, including it under the chapter entitled 'Environs of Ventnor'. He writes:

> The Esplanade is a noble drive and promenade, extending to the Coastguard Station. The northern section, beyond the Royal Spa Hotel, was built about ten years ago; the southern section in 1889. A new pier (to measure 1000 feet in length by 26 feet in width) is in course of construction.

Strange to say, Shanklin had no direct route to the centre of the Island until quite late on in its history. The journey to Newport, for example, meant travelling north to Lake and then turning left at The Stag Inn onto the Newport road via Alverstone. This was until the mid-1880s when Sibden Road was built leading through to the Whiteley Bank and thence onwards to Rookley and Newport. Built at a cost of £5,000, the Shanklin-Whiteley Bank Road opened in February 21st, 1885, and immediately shortened the distance to Newport by around half an hour. When soon afterwards came Queen Victoria's Diamond Jubilee, this was renamed Victoria Avenue on June 22nd, 1897. It is worth noting that today there is a new Sibden Road – a very recent creation on a modern housing development.

The days of the soft flickering of the yellow gas-lamp were numbered when, on July 19th, 1904, Shanklin's streets were illuminated at night-time by the steely eye of electricity for the first time. The lights were switched on by longshoreman Frank Rayner.

And so we have seen how, by 1900, Shanklin was well and truly on the map. It would accelerate until the outbreak of the First World War when visitations by foreigners largely ceased. It picked up in the decades before the start of the Second World War after which a combination of enemy action and the gradual increase in foreign travel and a change in the pattern of holidaying diminished demands and expectations. Let's just say that Shanklin today is not quite what it was.

The Esplanade

At the beginning of the 19th century, the waterfront below the cliffs was mostly a shelf of wasteland between Small Hope and The Chine and the Fisherman's Cottage. There were two or three cottages on it and a protective brief rudimentary sea wall. It seems that these were all erected between 1830 and 1840 and comprising Lincoln, Norfolk House and Osborne House. It was Norfolk House where Charles Darwin and his wife stayed in 1858.

Another cottage would be added by 1850 and this was that of the Preventive Officer – a lookout spot where smugglers might be detected and apprehended. By the time this was built the great days of the smuggler were drawing to a close. This building became the home of the local coastguard with a flagpole outside.

A pathway down the steep cleft in the cliff at Small Hope gave access to these cottages. A sea wall had been built to protect part of this path but it petered out midway along. The only regular access to the Esplanade was via Chine Hill. Rayner tells us that the deeds of the waterfront cottages had written into them the 'right to use Chine Hill'.

Before the coming of the railway in 1864, heavy goods transported to Shanklin had to come in by sea and, there being no pier yet, they had to be landed on the beach. The coal stores were where Beach Cottages would later be sited behind the Royal Spa complex, while timber was stored in racks situated under the cliff close to where the Lift would later be erected. There were partitioned-off areas for sacks of cement, fertiliser and piles of Welsh slates for roofing. Beach Cottages, built initially for hotel staff accommodation, were put up in 1872. In recent times they housed the headquarters of the local rowing club but, following a council report c.2011, they were swept away when a large site was needed to store materials in connection with the necessary extensive repairs to the then 50-odd year-old and troublesome concrete lift.

But we are ahead of the story. It was the work of one enterprising builder/developer that changed the face of the Esplanade. This was William Murley Summerhayes who set out to develop the Esplanade. In 1871-1872 he erected four houses at the centre point of the Esplanade and built a proper metalled road from Small Hope to them. These became what was first known as the Esplanade Hotel, later the Royal Spa Hotel and served to dominate the image of Shanklin for the next 65 or so years. His roadway was the first part of what eventually would be a completed Esplanade and sea wall.

Summerhayes went on to build a number of high-quality properties not just on the waterfront but also on the cliffs above. Eastcliff's Eton Lodge and Harrow Lodge were among the most notable and, unlike the Royal Spa Hotel, they survive to this day.

As the waterfront developed, there remained a long plot of wasteland under the cliff at the north end by Small Hope. Traditionally, this was where the holders of beach concessions might park their bathing machines for the winter months. This remained otherwise unused until after the pier was built. It seems that the coming of the pier was very much of a catalyst for the development of the Esplanade for after it was constructed and the Pavilion erected on it, entertainments began. This attracted important and experienced entrepreneurial impresarios. One of these was Powis Pinder.

After his own first appearance at the Pier Pavilion, entertainer Powis Pinder went on to play an important part in Shanklin entertainment. Camberwell-born Henry Powis Pinder (1872–1941) decided to stay in Shanklin with his wife Ethel and family, and from 1918 he staged burlesque evenings at the Town Hall and the Pier Theatre. Throughout the First World War, he ensured free tickets for all those wounded military personnel who were being treated in local military hospitals.

In 1919, Pinder's wooden stage and tented pavilion was destroyed by fire. He immediately bought a disused aircraft hangar from the waterfront at nearby Bembridge and had it re-erected on the wasteland where bathing machines were wintered. Originally used during the war by the Royal Naval Air Services, this hangar still stands on the Esplanade – much altered and today serving as an amusement arcade. Pinder set up on the Esplanade, fitting out the interior of the old hangar as an entertainment centre with a stage and proscenium. Named the Sunshine Theatre, it operated from 1921 to 1939. Here Pinder's company performed annual Sunshine concert parties which, in the early to mid-1930s, included artists such as singer Webster Booth and comedian Arthur Askey. The entertainers were chosen to try and trounce his rival Terry Wood with gagster Tommy Trinder at the Pier Pavilion and Casino.

The building of this theatre was first big change to the Esplanade after Summerhayes had built his hotel complex. After that, the remainder of the strip became a bowling green, tennis courts and tearooms. So it remained until the 1940s when a putting green was added. Today there are none of these activities which drew the holidaymaker to Shanklin in the Georgian days. They are all erased and replaced by a children's funfair.

Pinder and his family lived at Bay Tree Cottage, 169 Sandown Road. At the outbreak of the Second World War the theatre closed and was requisitioned as storage for Operation Pluto (Pipe Line Under The Ocean). Although he was by then 67, Pinder joined the local Auxiliary Fire Service as a volunteer eventually being promoted to Leading Fireman. He died the following year and received a full fireman's honoured funeral.

A significant event had occurred over the winter months of 1927-1928 which created a dramatic change to the appearance of the Esplanade. The council needed to revise the sewage system for the town and hit upon the idea of creating an effluent tank at the Small Hope end of the beach. Designed to blend in with the general shape of the sea wall, this was duly built and served the town until in post-war years a revised, modern method of treating sewage was introduced. The tank, however, remains to this day, only it is now filled up with inert rubble and employed as an extra parking area.

The presence of this extension to the waterfront breakwater and sea wall altered the shape and appearance of the Shanklin front but managed to achieve its goal without being too conspicuous or offensive.

With the coming of the war in 1939, many hoped that it would prove as harmless as was the First War to Shanklin, but this aspiration was cruelly shattered. The first German bomb to be dropped on Shanklin struck the Napier Hotel on the seafront and went off in the basement. Initially the building appeared intact but some minutes after the detonation the whole structure suddenly collapsed in a pile of rubble. Over the following war years, much of the Esplanade would be severely damaged by enemy bombing. Almost every property south of the pier was damaged to some extent, many extensively.

The Chine end of the Esplanade was to remain impassable well into the 1950s.

The biggest change to the post-war Esplanade was the decision to restore all the buildings but not the Royal Spa Hotel. While other buildings along the waterfront had been shattered, the big hotel remained extant and was capable of being reinstated. Instead, in 1956 it was demolished and the space turned into a huge car park. Never has there been a car park in such as prestigious position. It stood right opposite the entrance to the pier. The grand flagpole flew the Union Jack: there was no other ensign to flutter invitingly from the yardarm.

Gallant and sincere attempts to resurrect the pier were systematically thwarted, first by the gradual change in public tastes which meant that seaside entertainments were changing, and second by the escalating costs of maintenance and upkeep.

Matters were taken beyond mere personal endeavour on the night of October 15th-16th, 1987, when a massive storm decimated southern England. The pier, weakened by years of patch-up and lack of regular maintenance was already in parlous condition. The storm finished it off.

All that remained of the rich days of the past was the historic flagpole on its little arc of vegetation where the head of the pier had been. This pole survived until 2012 when the local council decided to cut it down.

Before the age of photography we relied upon the art of the engraver and his skills to give us reproductions of scenes and settings. The Isle of Wight was home to George Brannon who left us a masterful portfolio of wonderful engravings, many of Shanklin. He was not always absolutely accurate in his portrayals, the term 'artistic licence' being the ruling mantra. This view of the Chine, Fisherman's Cottage, Chine Inn and Lifeboat Station on what would later become the Esplanade is dated 1839 and was probably more of a representation than a detailed depiction. Those cliffs, for example…

This is an engraving published about 1850 by Kershaw & Co of London showing 'Shanklin Sands' looking south from somewhere near where the pier would be built half a century later on. The Fisherman's Cottage, visible in the upper picture, would be just out of sight round the corner of Chine Hill in the middle of this illustration.

What the Shanklin waterfront looked like before the development of the Esplanade. This very early photograph dates from about 1860 and shows the limit of Sea Terrace, precursor of the Esplanade, with the Preventive Station (forerunner of the Customs & Excise chaps) to the left. Access was purely by Chine Hill. Hope Hill had yet to be opened up.

The Fisherman's Cottage at the bottom of the Chine for much of its life seems to have been anything but the abode of a piscator! In this 1885 picture there is a prominent noticeboard on the north-facing wall reading 'Sampson's Warm Baths'. Efforts to date the cottage have proved largely unsuccessful but it was likely to have been built around 1811-1813. The Chine stream has carved out a meander in the beach in the foreground.

Shanklin Beach before the building of the pier, lift or other Esplanade features. The Royal Spa Hotel's two main buildings can be seen, here with their first and second-floor balconies extending inwards over the area where later would be built the four-peaked ogee-arched Conservatory and Palm Court. There is no flagpole. However, the cylindrical-section Summerhayes columns form the gateposts with their gas lamps on top. The hotel front wall contains two superimposed semi-circular cut-outs, one above the other, for dispensing the health-giving waters of the Spa spring to passers-by. The Esplanade roadway has not yet been completed, ceasing just opposite the hotel. The cliff path (Osborne Steps) has yet to be built behind the hotel. This is a rare picture dating from about 1875 and shows the hotel when it was relatively new and unexpanded.

A picture of the foreshore before the building of the Pier but after the Esplanade was extended beyond the Royal Spa Hotel. The stern of the second boat on the left bears the name of Edward Lale of Shanklin.

Spin forward some years. This clifftop view of the length of the Esplanade shows the newly-opened pier and, at the right, the Lift. The young trees on the far end of the roadway and the absence of the Jubilee Clock date the picture to the mid-1890s. In the foreground, left, is the vacant field where off-season parking was provided for bathing machines. Later this would be the site of the theatre and subsequent amusement arcade built by Powis Pinder.

Shortly before the turn of the century measures were put into action to try to retain the sand on Shanklin Beach and to prevent the tidal drift of beach material northwards. This remains a problem to this very day. For a long while Sandown had more sandy beaches than Shanklin where pebbles and stones greeted the visitor as he strove to traverse the foreshore for the water's edge at low tide. This was the era of the groyne – wooden palisades that formed a series of steps along the beach against which sand would be tide-drawn. The system worked and by 1910 most of our beaches had stout timber or stone groynes in place. Here one can be seen in the foreground.

Until its development, first with the re-erection of the RNAS Bembridge seaplane hangar which began as Powis Pinder's theatre and now serves as an amusement arcade, and then with bowling greens and tennis courts, the strip of land under the cliff face at the far end of the Esplanade by today's Hope Hill was open wasteland upon which bathing-machine proprietors were allowed to park their wheeled huts during the winter to get them off the beach. At the end of September each year the horses would take the machines, usually two at a time, along the Esplanade to the security of this storage ground. This picture was taken from the pier in 1906.

On the sands opposite the Royal Spa Hotel and next to the pier entrance, Fred Godfrey entertains holidaymakers in 1923. Godfrey – real name Llewellyn Williams – was a talented song-writer during the First World War and is remembered today for the songs *Take me back to dear old Blighty* (1916), and *Bless 'em All* (1917) which George Formby notably recorded in the 1940s. He was an accomplished and prolific musician and lyricist but after the war ended in 1918 his style of music gradually fell out of favour and by the mid-1920s this type of *al fresco* event increasingly became the only work he could get.

Shanklin Beach from the Pier in 1905 with the still quite new Jubilee Clock in view. This part of the foreshore was busy with more boats than bathing machines at this time as sea bathing had not yet achieved its popularity with the masses.

Photographed in the summer of 1908, the view south along the Esplanade shows the fully-developed roadway with the entrance to the pier on the left between the two octagonal kiosks, the Queen Victoria Diamond Jubilee Clock and, of course, the flagpole with its yardarm. Surmounting this is the triangular pennant reading 'HOTEL' while the yardarm displays the Union Jack.

Beneath Rylstone is the beach end of the Appley Steps down which the energetic, fit and intrepid might descend from the gardens above. This picture dates from 1913. Beach tents take the place of bathing machines at this end of the foreshore: they were easier and lighter to carry along the shore and erect.

By 1932 the Shanklin foreshore was a hive of activity, a good deal of it commercial as longshoremen made a living by hiring out rowing boats for 6d or 1/- an hour. The boats were numbered and, thanks to the Jubilee Clock on the Esplanade, checks could be kept on timing. Hence the once-common expression shouted from the shore 'Come in Number Seven!' There was always a good demand for deckchairs and the popular variety had folded canvas hood as well as canvas seats. They were less common after the war.

In this 1926 view of the Esplanade, the Napier Refreshment Rooms is to the left. Note the pillar box just past the entrance and outside the small post office which in those days stood on the site. Only a few of the trees planted along the waterfront have survived and have an inland 'set' from the prevailing on-shore wind. It is still an age when hat-wearing was *de riguer*.

People sometimes ask why the ceremonial clock was erected on the sea front instead of in the town itself. The answer is simple. There were no other clocks on the Esplanade and at that time few people carried pocket watches. Those who worked the bathing machines and others needed to know the time, especially those who hired out boats by the hour. A time indicator on the sea front was thus a blessing for many. This picture was taken at some time before 1910. The photographer was standing on the corner of the first-floor balcony of the Royal Spa Hotel to get this view.

Royal Spa Hotel

Originally known as the Esplanade Hotel, this was initially created as four houses at the centre of the distance between Small Hope cleft (later the location of Hope Hill) and the Chine. They were built by a man who greatly influenced the architecture of Victorian Shanklin, William Murley Summerhayes (1825-1895). It was he who planned the development of the Esplanade which, in the 1860s, was merely a sea wall and a few houses. Nearly all of these houses were let out as lodgings to visitors for the summer months. Norfolk House was rented out to Charles Darwin and his wife in 1858. Quite a number of the visitors were described as 'invalids', visiting the seaside in an attempt at seeking recovery from some illness or disease through 'the healthful exercise of sea-bathing' (Englefield: *Descriptions of… The Isle of Wight*).

Summerhayes was what would be called today a speculative builder. That he was so much more than that is proved by his popularity and the respect given him by Shanklin's residents when finally he departed the town.

Summerhayes' four houses comprised the Esplanade Hotel, Devonshire Villas, Glenelg and Templemore, all of which dated from 1871-1872 and would eventually coalesce into one establishment. Summerhayes was to erect a number of other buildings on the clifftop including Eton Lodge and Harrow Lodge. In the fullness of time and through some reason that has never been positively identified, Summerhayes over-extended himself and was bankrupted. He sold off everything he owned by auction and then emigrated with his family to New Zealand in 1875. Despite his obvious business failure and apparent humiliation, so great was the local respect for him that the ship on which he and his family departed diverted into the bay and the residents of Shanklin lined the clifftops and the Esplanade to wave him on his way.

The first licensee of what would quickly become The Royal Spa Hotel was none other than its builder, William Summerhayes in 1873. The following year (1874) the licence was transferred to Archibald Hinton.

Archibald Hinton (1815-1883) was no mere newcomer to the management of places having managed other attractions including London's Highbury Barn and Anerley Gardens. He had thus gained his experience at other spa venues in England. But he was also a twice-bankrupt, each time pulling himself out of financial chaos. One has to remember that bankruptcy was both all-too readily achieved and a great stigma to one's reputation. His misfortunes were not merely financial; his first wife, Charlotte Ann, died in 1852.

Hinton clearly liked Shanklin, the people – and his new hotel for he went out of his way to encourage society's upper crust to visit the town and to stay in his establishment. He is said to have kept a good supply of national flags so that a distinguished visitor always had his flag flying from the flagpole. After his death his aspirations were continued by others and the Royal Spa Hotel became the most prestigious establishment in the whole town. Even Hollier's and Daish's paled into, perhaps, not quite insignificance.

With the arrival of Queen Victoria and Prince Albert at Osborne on the northern coast of the Island, Shanklin had become a fashionable watering place. As well as our Royal Family, it was much frequented by European royalty which now eschewed Daish's and Hollier's for the Royal Spa, now called 'Hinton's Royal Spa Hotel', and its proximity to the sea.

In 1913, the Crown Prince of Germany stayed at the hotel while the following year found the Kaiser's youngest son, Prince Joachim, following suit. However when the threat of war with Germany reached the stage of an inevitability and with the start of the First World War just 24 hours away, he had to flee the hotel, the town – and the Island pretty rapidly. His rapid exit began by a high-speed ride to Ryde in Shanklin's first taxi driven by one Sid Hatcher.

The Royal Coat of Arms decorated the window of the Coffee House following visits from Queen Victoria's daughter, the Empress Frederick of Germany, and her brothers the Dukes of Edinburgh and Connaught. At the outbreak of the First World War, Victoria's son, Prince Heinrich of Prussia, brother of the Kaiser, was in residence and he, too, was forced to beat a hasty retreat.

A feature of the hotel was its so-called Winter Garden within which was its well-established grapevine growing up the front and then over the inside of the glazed roof. This gave a fine air and a sweet smell to the space which was furnished with Lloyd Loom woven-fibre chairs and tables.

There has long been known a book describing Shanklin in great detail and the Royal Spa Hotel in particular. Published in 1903 under the pseudonym of 'Monopole', this important work's true author has remained unknown until recently. For a long while it was suspected that it was penned by somebody with vested interests in the building. This suspicion was upheld when it was found recently that the author was none other than local mineral-water manufacturer and vendor and manager of the hotel after the Hinton era, Alfred Greenham.

Greenham's words, intended to be read as those of a mere outside observer, were thus selected for internal publicity. They are also accurate, if somewhat over the top.

> 'This Hotel deserves all that we can say of it for it is the Home of the Shanklin Spa. The Shanklin Spa is owned by the proprietors of this 'Royal' Hotel, it possesses the enormous

advantage of having a private entrance all under cover to the Baths, whilst part of the Spa Water is brought into the Winter Garden of the Hotel for the use of its visitors. The principal Hotel at Bath has this advantage, and I believe I have seen that it is claimed as a privilege existing nowhere else in England that this Hotel possesses medicinal baths. On the Continent at Aix La Chapelle, and Wiesbaden the Baths are within the Hotels which were built over the Springs, whilst Hinton's Royal Spa Hotel was built without reference to the Spa, and the Baths now adjoin the Hotel.

The Royal Spa Hotel has been patronised by the members of the Royal families of nearly every European country. The late Emperor Frederick of Germany, 'with our own Crown Princess,' the Empress Frederick visited the Hotel; so also have the Dukes of Edinburgh and Connaught. In the beautiful Coffee Room, the windows have the Coat of Arms of Royalty, for this is indeed a 'Royal' Room. It looks out into a Winter Garden of surpassing beauty and quite Continental in its appearance, one of the leading London papers describing it thus: — 'This Hotel is quite unique, there is nothing like it in the whole Isle of Wight. It looks from the sea like a fancy conservatory but on coming nearer we perceive that the central conservatory is really a lounge for winter and summer, separating and uniting the two wings of apartments. The management of the Hotel is simply perfect, the manageress being in every way an ideal one.' The Royal Spa Hotel is the only Hotel on the Esplanade, it is very picturesque in appearance, with all the principal rooms facing the sea.'

Sage words indeed! After the death of Archibald Hinton, his wife continued for a while but eventually the Hinton name ceased to be in the managerial role. For a number of years afterwards, the place retained the title 'Hinton's Royal Spa Hotel', this name being painted on the Summerhayes-featured cylindrical gate-posts.

After the passing of the Hinton management, the new chief was none other than Alfred Greenham – 'Monopole' no less.

The years between the two World Wars saw a decline in the hotel's visiting aristocracy and, with the passing of Queen Victoria back in 1901, there was a sharp decline in the popularity of the English Spa resorts. And Shanklin's reputation as a Spa town rapidly dwindled away.

This did not prevent the hotel being frequented by 'important' people and it remained a popular holiday venue for many until 1939. Thomas Beecham and Vaughan Williams were among the notable musicians that holidayed there.

On the outbreak of war, all stopped and the hotel was bombed, receiving several direct hits to the rear of the building, one of which destroyed the celebrated Baths. The Palm Court conservatory was also badly damaged. When the building behind was chosen to become one of the pump rooms for PLUTO, the entire ground floor of more than a third of the hotel complex was cleared and equipment installed. To avoid any tell-tale signs of this work being obvious from the aerial observation aircraft that the Luftwaffe regularly sent over to photograph the area, infinite care was taken not to clear bomb damage and to cover up any fresh wheel tracks from military vehicle activity.

At the end of the war, the building stood forlorn and empty, the roof signs reading 'Royal Spa Hotel' having been removed. It remained like this until 1955 when the Council decided to clear the site. Presumably nobody had come forward to repair and reinstate the place. For the season 1956, the Palm Court and Conservatory area was cleared along with the main or left-hand building and the right-hand side (the old Devonshire Villas) building opened as 'The Spa Bars' and painted in garish red and white.

At the end of the season, the whole complex was demolished and turned into a temporary car and coach park. It still serves that purpose nearly 70 years later.

An 1873 *carte de visite* by J B Middleton of Shanklin, of William Murley Summerhayes. It is the only known image of the developer who made the Esplanade and also built the Royal Spa Hotel. When he left Shanklin, crowds turned out to wave him off. Some builder!

The Royal Spa Hotel, erected by developer William Murley Summerhayes, was a barometer of Esplanade development. Much of the development of the shore-side can be gleaned from pictures of this sprawling building. Consisting of several houses joined (eventually) together, the hotel was also to become the most influential one in Shanklin – a staunch rival to the Old Village's Hollier's and Daish's. This circa 1880 view of Shanklin Beach shows the Royal Spa Hotel's two main buildings in their first form with the balconies extending inwards over where the Palm Court or Conservatory would be erected later. The promenade and sea wall stops opposite the hotel and the beach extends up to the walls of the gardens of subsequent waterfront buildings.

Looking north along the Esplanade in about 1887 just before work on building the pier began. The Royal Spa Hotel has just completed its Palm Court and the adjacent buildings have their balconies cut back to eliminate the inwards-facing portions. The flagpole stands on the opposite side of the metalled roadway and Moorman's bathing machines are where the Pier will be erected. A rowing-boat lies across the pavement, extreme right, near where the Jubilee Clock will be erected thirteen years later. Newly-planted trees can be seen on the right side.

This photograph from about 1890 shows the great hotel in its early days with the newly-built glass house between the two main buildings. The name of the hotel is displayed in its original form painted on boards: individual letters would appear later along with the 'coat of arms' feature. The cylindrical gateposts surmounted by gas lamps bear the name 'Hinton's Royal Spa Hotel' to promote the management of Archibald Hinton. The main entrance to the building is at the extreme left. The two semi-circular 'windows' in the hotel wall, right, where passers-by might sample the spring water piped from the spring in the cliffs at the rear of the hotel.

The Royal Spa Hotel after its extensive remodelling of the centre building and its Conservatory and Palm Court. The main hotel building on the left now displays the faux 'coat of arms' fixed above the word 'Spa' that Hinton created to appeal to his high-ranking clientele. Note that the flagpole stands in the front garden of the hotel. This would later be moved across the road to the pavement outside the entrance to the pier.

The pier opened at the end of the 1891 season. This picture, taken soon after it was completed, shows all the boats arranged neatly on the foreshore. The shed more or less in line with the also newly-built Osborne Steps displays on its roof the words 'Blew's Bathing & Boating Office'. Ted Blew was a longshoreman and this was his 'extra' business. Ultimately his business was absorbed by Moorman. Keats Inn is visible on the top of the cliffs at the left. The wind-break sun-lounge is part way down the Osborne Steps. The Royal Spa Hotel's Coat of Arms above the left side main building is missing – probably a result of storm damage or even re-painting.

Taken from a low-flying aircraft, here is the Royal Spa Hotel in about 1928. The front door to the hotel is at the extreme left by the entry to Osborne Steps. Gone are the two columns surmounted by gas lamps. The flagpole, which originally stood in the hotel forecourt, is now positioned across the road at the small flower bed that formed the entrance to the pier. Here it would remain until cut down by council workers at the end of 2012. Behind the main building on the left is the ballroom with its access to the Osborne Steps and, behind that, the staff accommodation house. Today every one of these buildings has gone, the site becoming a huge car-park.

The wall surrounding the Royal Spa Hotel had two places for drinking fountains. These allowed people to have a free sample of the mineral-rich spring water upon which the hotel's fame rested. Unfortunately, so great was the solids content of the water that the pipes which served this facility soon clogged up. The free fountains were removed but the decorative wall remained a feature for a very long while. This photo shows the second of the hotel's main buildings. The white sign protruding shows that the hotel was approved by the Automobile Association — 'AA Recommended'.

This photograph, below, was taken in June 1950. The hotel is now derelict, the conservatory gone and many windows glassless. The pier, partially opened that year after a shoestring 'restoration', now has incomplete lamp-standards made out of patent Dexion slotted steel angle. The lanterns have yet to be fitted. Within four years, demolition would start on the hotel, the right hand building surviving as a cut-down white and red painted structure named Spa Bars. The site of the old Conservatory was given over to open-air seating. It was not a hotel anymore and the clientele was definitely not the same. The following year would see the whole site cleared creating the most prestigiously placed car-park.

Pictured in 1890 from a place where the Lift access bridge would be built the following year, this view of Keats Green shows Keats Inn right of centre. The Summerhayes-built houses on the clifftop all had the characteristic pineapple-topped cylindrical gate posts as seen here on Harrow Lodge. The pineapple was a popular contemporary decoration, a legacy from the 17th century when it was King Henry III's cherished object, the fruit having just been introduced into Britain from Holland, his homeland.

From 1948 comes this picture of Keats Green taken from the path down from the Lift with the twin cylindrical stone gateway columns of Eton Lodge right of centre and Keats Inn's garden prospect above. The hydrangeas for which Shanklin's clifftop was renowned suffered damage and neglect during the war years and their post-war display was not as rich and generous as in the heady days of the 1930s.

A long-time feature of the clifftop is Keats Inn, one of Shanklin's more unusual examples of Victorian architecture. Originally built in 1878 as the Shanklin Gentlemen's Club – an identity that it maintained until around 1896 – the unknown architect drew heavily on Gothic and Mughal styles for his creation. Rich in detailing in concrete, cast iron and wood, the building stands prominently on a sloping site and has an unusual half-hipped roof with intensively decorated and fretted bargeboards. But it is the side facing the sea and the end gables which display the most distinctive features. Three blind *occuli* on the front display a simple motif repeated on the open gable and the hipped gable. The front shows two that are quatrefoil while the centre one is trefoil. The end ones are similar but all four-lobed. For more than a century this fine building served as a pub and hotel and was a popular venue with holidaymakers and courting couples for the vistas from its secluded garden. Granted Grade II Listed status in 1990, in recent years it has been converted into private flats.

The clifftops have always been remembered for their rich display of hydrangeas. None of the properties fronting the sea actually extended to the edge of the cliff. This was a legacy from when customs officers and coastguards needed a continuous coastline view of potential smugglers at sea. The Island was once a rich venue for smugglers and Shanklin was high up on the list of defaulters, largely due to the proximity of the Continent and the inordinately large numbers of shipwrecks around its coast. This view is from a picture-postcard by Photo-Precision Ltd of St Albans who were in business from 1946 to 1969. Judging from the original gas lamp-standard converted to electricity with its mirror-wing reflectors, the picture must date from after 1950.

Shanklin foreshore in 1923 showing the bottom of the Chine and the Fisherman's Cottage. The white shed, centre, bears the name Pike. This was Mrs E F D Pike who had a business taking photographs of holidaymakers on the Esplanade. The pictures were of the 'tintype' style where a cameraman with a wooden tripod would expose his image using a special type of camera. The very thin emulsion-coated metal plate would then be dropped into a rubber bag hung beneath the camera where it would be developed for two minutes, taken out and dried and then presented to the subject in exchange for 4d or 6d. Tintypes were seldom permanent images unless separately chemically fixed. The majority were not and would gradually darken over the months that followed. Also known as ferrotype pictures, these were still popular on Shanklin front until the outbreak of war after which they were quite forgotten with the advance of 35mm film cameras.

Former home of the White Popham family, the Manor House is now a hotel. This view from just before the war shows its garden side. Francis White Popham (1829-1894) was the last Lord of the Manor and carried out extensive alterations to the old Manor House, adding two wings to the side of the main building and also the entrance porch. After his death, the estate passed to his wife, Margaret, Lady Hatherton, and then his sister, Mary Popham White, later Popham-Macpherson. The family still own extensive property in Shanklin, including Shanklin Chine, through Anne Springman (née Macpherson), Francis' great-great niece. The house was bought by the council before the First World War with much of the land put into public ownership. The house itself was sold on to the Workers' Travel Association (WTA) as a hotel for the underprivileged and then turned into a luxury hotel in 1979. Extensively renovated and restored to its former glory, today it comprises self-catering holiday apartments.

The Pier

When the Cowes-built paddle steamer *Gem* owned by the Isle of Wight Steam Packet Company visited Shanklin on July 10th, 1858, she dropped anchor off the shore and took her passengers ashore by rowing boat. It was all a bit of a chore and one which would have been greatly simplified had there been a pier.

The earliest proposal for a pier was in 1864 when the Shanklin Bay Pier Company received a Board of Trade order for a 1,200-foot long pier. This came to nothing and the company failed. A further attempt by a new Shanklin Pier Company in 1877 also collapsed. Its proposals had not pleased everybody and the Revd Edmund Venables, a respected local cleric, had spoken out against it. In 1860 he wrote:

> A very few years since, Shanklin was perhaps the loveliest village in the Isle of Wight... But now, alas! All is changed or fast-changing... the retired village has swelled into the fashionable watering-place, and the watering-place greed of gain is making itself painfully manifest.

To rub salt into the wounds of those who believed that the future demanded a boat landing stage, Shanklin's then-arch rival of Sandown had gone ahead and built its own pier – admittedly a low-budget slender affair costing £6,000, just 360 feet in length and supported on spindly minimalist iron columns – but a pier all the same.

In 1877 a new company was formed – Shanklin Pier Company Ltd. Capitalised at £8,000 with 1,600 shares each worth £5. A list of directors and shareholders revealed three notable names – John Daish (of the eponymously-named hotel), Archibald Hinton (proprietor of The Royal Spa Hotel) and C H Moorman who leased skiffs, motor boats, rowing boats and beach-chairs to the visitors.

The first design was rejected but in December 1880 fresh plans gained momentum. Sadly there was still a vociferous bunch of local protestors who did not want a pier. Prominent amidst these objectors was none other than the well-respected local landowner and Lord Mayor, Francis White Popham. These objections created delays and by the time the Pier Construction Bill went before Parliament, the Shanklin Pier Company Ltd found itself bereft of capital and quickly went the way of its predecessors. On September 3rd, 1886, it ceased to be. Sandown smirked...

Its collapse coincided with the formation of a third company – the Shanklin Esplanade & Pier Company (SE&PC) incorporated on December 22nd, 1885, with a capital of £12,000. Archibald Hinton was by now dead. This new company was made of sterner stuff than its predecessors and it started construction of a pier in August of 1888.

The task took two years to complete and the finished structure was not opened until August 18th, 1890. It had cost £24,000 – four times the price Sandown had spent some years earlier when it erected its first rather utilitarian pier.

The new Shanklin Pier was a simple, unadorned platform over the sea, its entrance on the Esplanade opposite The Royal Spa Hotel, sporting two small turreted ticket-offices, one to each side. There were no wind-breaks or other structures along the length of the pier. Two landing jetties were placed at the pierhead, arranged as an arrowhead so that paddle steamers could be docked regardless on the direction of wind and tide. At the shore end was the historic flagpole, relocated from the front garden of the Royal Spa Hotel and now placed centrally at the pier entrance. This flagpole with its yardarm had, according to Fred Mew, been one of the masts salvaged from a ship that had foundered on Dunnose.

Early on it was decided to build a pavilion halfway along the pier where people could gather for a dance or variety show. This was duly built and opened on July 28th, 1909. The first show was 'The Burlesques' run by 'Bunny' Bennett. The cast included Connie Crighton and the singers husband and wife Powis Pinder. This enterprise did not last long, though, for late in the evening of June 29th, 1918, and after everybody had gone home, the pavilion was found to be on fire. Late revellers watched it burn down. Despite an investigation the cause of the fire remained uncertain although it was more than likely due to a carelessly discarded cigarette end. For some years afterwards, the middle of the pier displayed the skeletal remains of this building. A local builder removed some of the unspoiled steel girders and in 1920 used them to build the town's first cinema – the Playhouse.

With the privations of the First World War and a fall in the number of holidaymakers, the pier company was extremely stretched in funds and could not afford to rebuilt the gutted pavilion. The most that could be afforded was the repair of burned decking.

Steamers no longer called at the pierhead because back in March of 1916 the jetties were removed after sustaining storm-damage

And so the years went by with the partial steel frame of the pavilion still standing – certainly a blot on the environment – and no steamers calling with money-spending passengers. The pier steadily rotted away only providing for those who wanted to walk it or from enterprising fishermen with their own stools upon which to sit.

In was in this sorry state that in 1925 it passed into the hands of Terry Wood. The man with the odd name – his surname was Terry Wood without the hyphen –

was lessee of the Theatre Royal in Ryde. Horace Terry Wood (1889-1959) bought the derelict pier at a knock-down price with the idea of restoring it. His first task was to build a new pavilion.

A new much enlarged pavilion opened on June 4th, 1927. Called The Casino it seated 1,000 people and heralded a long and successful period as a Shanklin entertainment venue. That opening night saw comic characters including 'Professor' Howe, a Punch and Judy show and the Isle of Wight Minstrels. The building included a ballroom which would be the venue for the entertainment 'Dancing over the Sea' for almost 40 years.

Numerous star acts of the time performed there. In 1929, Terry Wood featured his 'Cabaret Kittens' to follow the previous year's 'Casino Follies'

As Terry Wood's pier pavilion thrived, he continued with the pier restoration, renewing the pierhead landing stages which opened for business in May 1931. Meanwhile, artists who appeared at the pavilion included the top-liners of the time such as Arthur Askey, Elsie and Doris Waters, Cyril Fletcher, Flotsam and Jetsam, Richard Tauber, Pavlova, Tommy Trinder and Paul Robeson. There were also appearances by Clarkson Rose with his Twinkle ensemble, Sophie Tucker and Barney Powell who was so taken with Shanklin that he moved his family there and, besides becoming a regular on the local entertainment programme, opened his once-famous Barney's Emporium shop off the High Street.

It was not all plain-sailing, though, and Terry Wood was to find out that there was more to running a seaside show than just building a venue and taking the money. One Sunday pier show saw him end up in Court. An undercover police officer named Lewis attended the evening entertainment on June 27th, 1937 and, as a result, Terry Wood was prosecuted, appearing before a magistrate under Section 3 of the Sunday Entertainment Act. The double-act comedians Clapham and Dwyer were said to have told 'unsuitable' jokes while Tommy Trinder, notorious for his on-stage risqué monologues, was alleged to have told 'unseemly' stories. Terry Wood was fined £10 and urged to redouble his efforts to abide by the strict Sunday entertainment guidelines in the future.

Even so, Trinder was to spend three consecutive summers at the Pier show. Terry Wood also signed up musicians who were at the top of their profession at the time. Among the dance bands were Jack Payne, Jack Hilton, Harry Gold and Billy Cotton. 'Dancing over the Sea' was the slogan used to advertise these events and the regular band was Eric Hill and his Musicians.

In May of 1931, a second, smaller dancehall was opened at the pierhead which included 'Terry's Bar'. In 1938, Anthony Eden, who went on to become Britain's Foreign Minister and then Prime Minister, was a welcome visitor to that nightspot. The landing stages vied for steamers as once again they were encouraged to put Shanklin on their destinations. Boats now toured the Island, taking holidaymakers for cruises. The fare for round the island was 6/6d or to Cherbourg and back 15/-.

The 'thirties saw a continual expansion of pier activities and consequent profits. But all was not to last as the clouds of war gathered. With the outbreak of the 1939-1945 war, everything changed and Shanklin Pier's entertainment stopped instantly.

Very quickly an amazing steel balustrade was erected around the south and east coasts of Britain including the Isle of Wight. The nation's coastal defences were considered impregnable. All along the South coast and up the Eastern seaboard beach defences comprising tightly bolted together steel tubular scaffold provided a hazard to all invaders while all seaside piers were cut, each having a section removed so that if an invader thought he could land at one (and, presumably, get past the locked turnstile at the shore end), he would not get very far. Many fine piers were unnecessarily spoiled in this way, Shanklin being no exception.

There was, however, an ironic twist to the story. Part of our planned invasion of enemy-occupied Europe involved getting a supply of petrol across the Channel to keep tanks, vehicles and aircraft based there operational. So was conceived PLUTO – Pipe Line Under The Ocean. The aim was to create a continuous pipeline from fuel depôts in Central England all the way to France. The Isle of Wight was to be the 'jumping-off' point and that would centre on Shanklin.

Pumping stations in the Chine, at the Royal Spa Hotel and Sandown's Brown's Golf Course would feed petrol down the pier and thence under the sea to France. There was only one problem – a necessary part of the pier had been removed!

A slender steel bridge was built between the two halves strong enough to take the weight of the pipeline and to serve as a crossing for one man at a time. Post-war picture postcards show this and also the various stages at trying to close up the two parts once Peace had been reinstated.

The war took its toll on many things and by the end of the conflict the pier was in extreme dereliction. All the lamp standards and their Victorian globes had gone. As things opened up again in the late 1940s, parts of the pier were re-opened, but there were missing deck planks and other areas fenced off for safety. Utility lamp standards were erected made of Dexion, that handy patented bronze-coloured slotted angle iron that was so popular for making shelving and benches. It looked 'make-do-and-mend': it was.

Summer shows continued for several years, and in one of them '50s pop star Anne Shelton topped the bill. The pier continued its pre-war 'Dancing over the Sea' events.

The immediate post-war years found the pier the centrepiece of an extraordinary legal case. Part of Terry Wood's extensive renovation work called for the painting of the structure in an attempt to stem the deterioration which had accelerated during the war years. A paint company was contracted to do the job using a new substance 'guaranteed to last seven to ten years'. Sadly the claims made for the paint were to prove false and within three months of application the stuff began to peel off. Terry Wood sued the firm.

Meanwhile pier entertainments went on and in 1949-1950 one could dance at the pierhead to the toe-tapping music of Jimmy Leach and his Organolians. Because the Sunday Observance laws were still strictly adhered to, Sundays were given over to band concerts.

Terry Wood's sudden death in 1959 transferred the operation of the pier to his wife, Sadie. She retired in 1970 putting the pier up for sale at £85,000. There were several subsequent owners who came and went, the pier's deterioration continuing more or less unchecked.

1976 saw a new owner, an energetic local businessman called Fred Sage who had great hopes for the venue. He was also a founder member of the National Piers Society. Among the events staged was a live television programme in 1980 and a show starring Cardew 'The Cad' Robinson, Norman Vaughan and Peggy Mount. Barney Powell, who almost half a century earlier had trodden the boards with Clarkson Rose, was also on the stage, together with the Isle of Wight's own jazz group, the popular 'Temperance Seven'. It was a TV show that everybody watched and it earned Fred Sage important and much-valued revenue.

But Sage's enthusiasm was now feeling the strain of mounting expenditure to keep the pier going. Salvation seemed in sight when the pier and its buildings together with the two original Esplanade kiosks, were granted Grade II Listed Building status. Sage now sold out to a fresh company in which he held a 25 percent stake.

The night of October 15th-16th, 1987, brought the terrible hurricane that devastated much of Southern England. It was the most severe storm in living memory. An estimated 15 million trees were blown down. And, in the morning, most of the pier was gone, spread as wreckage along the sands from Dunnose to Sandown. The pier was not insured.

In 1993 the council paid a contractor £189,000 to remove the remains of the 103-year old structure. Only the historic flagpole and yardarm remained. In 2012, the council felled that and took it away.

August 18th 1890 and the new pier is finished and open for the first time. The crowds flock to relish the thrill of walking out over the sea. A paddle steamer has moored at one of the arrowhead jetties at the pierhead. The bunting and the flags are out for the occasion.

This photograph shows the newly-opened pier which was inaugurated on August 18th, 1890. The absence of the Lift in this view means that it was taken before the Spring of 1891. There are no shelters on the pier and the Jubilee Clock is still nine years away in the future. A fine view of the gas lamp which illuminated the walkway is seen on the left with its Berringer glass globe. Next to it on the horizon is the spire of the recently completed St Saviours Church close to Keats Green and the architecturally unusual Gentlemen's Club which later would become Keats Inn.

The paddle steamer *Lorna Doone* pulls away from the pier in 1906 probably en route for Bournemouth. The triangular flag pennant on the shoreside end displays the word 'Hotel' advertising the Royal Spa Hotel. This rather poor snapshot was taken from halfway up Osborne Steps.

A 1905 view of Shanklin Pier showing its initial style devoid of all but windbreak sun lounges strategically placed along its length and the small gable-roofed ticket shed and waiting room at the pierhead where onward tickets could be bought by those who wanted to board a paddle steamer for a cruise to Bournemouth or Southsea. In the foreground is the newly-completed Jubilee Clock.

Looking down the pier at the newly-completed pavilion opened in the summer of 1909. This structure would survive until 1918 when it burned down. Prominent in this 1910 picture is the tower of St Saviours-on-the-Cliff, left of centre. Town gas was pumped from the gasworks by the railway at Shanklin's Landguard Road to the cast iron lamps in the foreground with their Berringer glass globes. Barely visible at the right and through the aegis of sympathetic design is the Newnes' Hydraulic Lift linking waterfront with town.

From 1913 comes this view of the pier showing the first Pavilion opened in 1909. Numerous other buildings have appeared along the length of the structure. The structure has acquired some more supporting piles and bracings.

This view of the pier was taken in the autumn of 1918 just after the first pavilion had been destroyed by fire. Its blackened skeletal remains are clear to see. Some postcard makers sought to retouch their old cards by 'removing' the ruined pavilion.

This snapshot was taken in the spring of 1927 and shows the Pier with its new and enlarged pavilion. The Pierhead has now lost its mooring jetties for embarking passengers from visiting paddle steamers. These were taken away in 1918 and would not be replaced until 1931. As a consequence, no steamers called at Shanklin for 13 years! Not a wise move for business, but the heydays of the resort were already in the past and the two decades between the two wars saw no more visits from foreign nobility and the aristocracy ; they had discovered other places to holiday. Why, you could now fly to India in four days! The picture was taken from Keats Green .

Dating from April 1938 is one of the last pre-war images of the pier showing its extended pavilion, known as The Casino, and pierhead buildings with arrowhead jetties for visiting steamers. Other buildings housing fairground-type sideshows have appeared on the structure. Pierhead jetties meant steamers could once more visit Shanklin.

Photographed from the upstairs corner window of the second pier pavilion, the view back along the pier to the Esplanade is seen in this picture postcard from July 1914. It shows the imposing presence of the Royal Spa Hotel and reveals the Lift at the right. Cut-out letters framed over the pier entrance read IDEALS, the meaning of which is now lost. Shelters and wind-breaks are starting to proliferate on the walkway.

At the outbreak of the 1939-1945 war, the progress of Nazi Germany through Europe appeared to pose a very real threat of invasion to Britain and, in the belief that the invaders would arrive in a traditional, gentlemanly way, ie. one up from a paddle-steamer but nevertheless by boat, it was decided that all South and East Coast seaside piers would be taken out of commission by having a section blown up by the Royal Engineers. Shanklin Pier was no exception. Only afterwards, when PLUTO (Pipe Line Under The Ocean) was planned was it realised that Shanklin Pier was really needed to play a vital part in the transportation of fuel to our invasion forces. PLUTO had three separate sites just in case one or even two became incapacitated. The first was the Chine, the second was the Royal Spa Hotel and Pier, and the third Brown's Golf Course at the Culver end of the Sandown waterside. The upshot was the provision of a slender suspension bridge erected across the chasm to carry the pipe across the gap to the Pierhead. This temporary wartime construction is visible at the right of this 1945 photograph

A picture postcard from 1945 before the pier was partially re-opened to the public. The gap cut by the Royal Engineers in 1942 is clear to see as is the remedial bridge they then had to build to carry the necessary PLUTO pipeline to the pierhead.

Taken in 1952, this view of the pier shows the 'second-stage' in-fill of the cut-away section beyond the pavilion which is categorised by having numerous concrete piles in the sea. Such a volume of concrete in the sea would have created enormous resistance to tidal flow let alone storm tides. This structural oversight would survive until the 1987 storm. Clearly seen in the left foreground is the angular outline of the effluent tank built in 1928 and forming the southern-most boundary of Small Hope Beach.

October 15th-16th 1987 was the night of the Great Storm which devastated all of southern England. Wind speeds in excess of 122 mph felled an estimated 15 million trees. Shanklin Pier, already derelict but several years into active consideration for restoration, took the full force of the storm, and winds combined with huge waves ravaged the 98-year-old structure. The foreground section is the concrete-built part beyond the pavilion which has now disappeared along with the whole of the end of the structure and the landing stages. At the top of the picture is the now-vacant site once occupied by the Royal Spa Hotel. A sight-seeing motor-coach is parked where the great Palm Court and Conservatory once fronted the billiards room. The beaches of Sandown Bay were strewn with wreckage from the pier, parts of the pavilion being identified as far away as Brown's Golf Course beyond Sandown. The remains of the old structure would now be cleared away and Shanklin would no more have a pier nor entertainments such as 'Dancing over the Sea'.

Shanklin Esplanade with no Jubilee Clock on the waterfront while the Royal Spa has its flagpole positioned at the entrance to the Pier. Far right, the Lift is visibly under construction, the upper access bridge still being framed before cladding. The Lift cars are absent. The picture thus dates from 1889-90.

A picture postcard mailed in 1932 shows a similar view, this time taken from half a mile closer to the Chine Inn and showing the roof of the Fisherman's Cottage in the right foreground. The tortuous Appley Steps down the cliff can just be made out right of centre. The shape of the headland changed over the years as coastal erosion brought repeated rock falls. The liquid 'blue slipper' clay continually leached from these hefty rocks in sinuous, sticky rivulets, an indication that they were unsteady.

Newnes' Hydraulic Lift

Shanklin had its limitations, which were of a geographical nature. Effectively existing on two levels, the town was separated from the shore by a steep cliff. One had to walk round this escarpment to get down to the waterfront, either by a track at the Small Hope (Sandown) end or by an even more difficult path close to the Chine. When it came to developing the area as a holiday resort, there were obvious problems.

First was the improvement of the Small Hope access by the creation of a zigzag roadway down which horses and carts could travel from the railway station to the hotels and guest houses on the Esplanade. A fully-laden horse and cart could not make the journey down without two men with wheel chocks for the front wheels to prevent the cart driving its horses and running away. Travelling back up the hill meant slackening the reins and again having two people to chock the rear wheels.

It was clear that there had to be an alternative way of travelling up and down from the Esplanade. While visitors with luggage would continue with horse-drawn transport with all its limitations until the invention of the motor car and motor bus, ordinary people on foot needed better access betwixt town and Esplanade. During the 1880s several proposals were made regarding installing a Lift.

The earliest of these was in 1881 with the formation of The Shanklin Lift Company. This firm came and went, leaving nothing behind. None other than Magnus Volk (1851-1937) who was in the early days of his career which had begun with his electric railway in Brighton in 1883, put forward a scheme for a lift in 1884. On April 28th he presented a proposal for a passenger lift near the coastguard hut on the Esplanade.

The council approved his proposal, but from that point onwards the Volk proposition goes dark and disappears. Given Volk's background in electricity, it would probably have been electrically operated which makes us think it would also have needed a powerful steam engine to generate power and consequently demand a fairly stiff investment not to mention high operational costs.

All was quiet until along came the man who not only knew about cliff lifts but had the wherewithal to make such a feature happen. This was the publisher and philanthropist George Newnes (1851-1910). Born the same year as Volk, Newnes was a self-made businessman, polymath, visionary and inventor. The newspaper proprietor, who founded *The Strand Magazine*, *Country Life* and *Tit-Bits*, had already created the Lynton to Lynmouth Cliff Railway that linked the two towns for the first time. He also proposed the Babbacombe to Oddicombe Cliff Railway, not actually built until as late as 1923.

It was the Lynton-Lynmouth cliff railway that was most promising. A combination of funicular railway and balanced lift, its operation was simple, effective and cheap. It made use of water-balanced cars which operated silently up and down the steep rock slope that separated the two towns.

This was a fine example for a similar structure in Shanklin although instead of the two cars running up and down a steep cliff railway, they would hang free and operate vertically like a lift in a tower. Proposals came and went as time flew by…

Despite a nervous council that procrastinated on the grounds of probable costs, the people of Shanklin pressed for action. On January 6th, 1891, the council rejected the latest proposal citing spiralling costs. It was at this point that George Newnes, not knighted until 1895, stepped forward and, flushed with the success of his West Country engineering, offered to finance the Shanklin Lift project. The council, aware of the downside to eyeing gift horses in the mouth, acted quickly and the plans for the Lift were approved on February 3rd, 1890. Without the backing of Sir George Newnes, it is unlikely the project would ever have got off the ground.

Construction began at a point on Eastcliff Promenade opposite Harrow Lodge above Eton Lodge with their instantly recognisable Summerhayes' twin-columned gateways on the corner nearest Keats Green. The Lift was completed and opened in time for the end of the 1891 season and was reputed to have cost £4,000.

The purchase of the property was made in 1893 by the Shanklin Lift Co. 4205 shares were allocated. Newnes himself held 4,000 shares and, at a meeting on July 31st, 1893, the conveyance of the Lift to the company was signed and sealed.

Operation of the Lift was by means of simple, foolproof hydraulics – each of the two cars which could carry 40 people at a time had a hollow bottom which was a water tank. For every journey, the water load in the lower car was balanced by the load in the top car and once that was established, the brake was released and the car would slowly and silently rise as the upper one descended. It was only necessary to release a small volume of water from the lower car to set it in motion. The heavier car at the top then descended, allowing the lower, lighter car to ascend.

Each of the two cars weighed 35cwt when empty and up to 5 tons when full. The rope that united them was designed to hold weights in excess of 40 tons. Passenger facilities included red-tiled waiting rooms and lavatories, as well as a 'National Telephone Company' office from which phone calls could be made'.

A notable feature of the George Newnes Lift was that it was entirely skeletal with a slender cable-braced rectangular-sectioned frame. Apart from a red-tiled roof turret to house the winding machinery, the Lift tower was no more than a slender open structure. Extending 130 feet up the rock face, it was not obtrusive, it blended with its surroundings and it was attractive in appearance.

Around the mid-1920s the cable-braced sides of the Lift tower were replaced by slender steel strips to counter a slight sway which was apparently detectable in strong winds.

Operating the Lift involved two men, Harry Lavender and George Oatley. One began his working day at the top and the other at the bottom and they each worked an 80 hour week. The minutes of a meeting of the Lift Company for May 8th 1939 records the Chairman reporting that Harry Lavender was now in his 73rd year and was working 106 hours per week.

To keep the Lift operational when there might not be sufficient numbers of passengers going the other way, a 14 hp Crossley gas engine powered pumps which lifted sea water to the clifftop where it was stored in a 12,000 gallon tank. A similar tank was used to store fresh water which was tapped from springs in the cliff. Once the descending car reached the bottom of the shaft, two hydraulic rams released the water from the car which was then pumped back to the top.

During the war the Lift was used for military purposes and the lift suffered damage from this and enemy action. Post war it remained derelict until taken over by the Sandown-Shanklin UDC Act of 1955. Rather than repair the old Lift, it was decided to demolish it and build a modern electric one.

In the spring of 1957, George Newnes' old Lift was pulled down and a new one of reinforced concrete electrically operated was built at a cost of some £16,000. It opened on May 14th 1958 and ran from Easter to early November.

On a Royal Visit to the Isle of Wight in 1965, Queen Elizabeth and the Duke of Edinburgh rode the new Lift down to the Esplanade from the town on July 26th.

The new Lift began to give cause for concern toward the end of the 20th century and weaknesses appeared to show up in its modern technology which allowed independent operation of the two 'carriages'. Each of the two carriages was said to be able to carry 40 people and travel the 112 feet up or down the cliff in 33 seconds.

In March of 2015, because of concerns about the condition of the metal bridge at the top of the cliff, the Lift was closed and the bridge taken away while a new one was made and fitted. This work proved extensive and expensive and kept the Lift shut until the following Easter. A temporary bridge then had to be installed while more 'permanent' remedies were sought. It was then realised that almost all the original machinery from the 1950s was in need of replacement. As none of the required parts for the original Lift were made or stocked anywhere, an even more extensive modernisation programme than had been expected began. The cost of this overhaul was in excess of £700,000 by the time the Lift re-opened in June 2016.

Then, following a series of technical faults, it was closed for repairs to be carried out on one of the two carriages. These, hampered by difficulties in sourcing spares, kept the Lift shut until mid-2016. The council said upgrade works were hit by 'numerous challenges'. These included a difficulty in sourcing parts for the structure. All, though, was not right and so, on Sunday, September 1st 2019, three people were trapped in one of the capsules when there was a power failure. Firemen had to winch the carriage to the ground by hand before they could open the doors and release 'two customers and an employee'.

Once more the simple reliability of the 1892 Lift and its engineering was highlighted.

A picture taken shortly before the First World War. While the paddle steamers were shallow-draft boats, the rise of screw-driven ships really called for a greater depth of water and soon the Pier would be extended into deeper water at low tide. On the right is a detailed view of the head of the Lift showing one car at the top.

With the 20-20 vision of hindsight it can be seen how George Newnes' hydraulic lift merged into the Shanklin scenery so effortlessly. Artistic, stylistically pleasing and blending well with its surroundings. This view of the Lift head shows the bridge and the waiting room/ticket-office cabin. One lift cabin has just begun its descent. The two ladies in the foreground are dressed in fineries complete with complicated hats. This picture was taken from Keats Green in 1906.

Taken from Osborne Steps, this view of the Lift reveals its slender proportions and somewhat minimalistic construction. The two cars are have just passed one another. The winding gear in the tiled canopy is partly visible. Left foreground is the shelter part way down the Steps.

Not a particularly good snapshot but a rare one looking up from the cliff bottom at the Lift. One of the stay cables extends from the left of the upper portion. Several of these discretely braced the tower to the cliff face.

Another unusual angle for a picture, this time a view taken from the Eastcliff Promenade along the clifftop to the head of the Lift. Note how pleasingly it fits in with the architecture of its surroundings. The small glazed cabin on the bridge between cliff edge and the Lift itself was painted green to reflect its environment. Just visible above the cabin is one of those horizontal steel cables that braced the tower to the cliff face.

Queen Victoria's Jubilee Clock

On June 22nd, 1897, the nation celebrated the 60th year of the reign of Queen Victoria. For her, however, it wasn't much of a cause for festivity for she had been in mourning for her dear Prince Albert since his death some 35 years or so earlier. It was almost as if her people were a separate entity, for they would celebrate wildly up and down the country while the subject of their adulation was anything but in the mood to mark the occasion.

The celebrations were many and varied. Towns and villages usually went in for something substantial that would stand the test of time or bear a suitable dedication. It had all started with the Golden Jubilee year a decade earlier. For that event, Ryde named a new children's wing at the Isle of Wight Infirmary and County Hospital and went one step further, commissioning a new pipe-organ for its own town hall. This was opened by a recital given by the Island's own internationally famed organist and composer, Ventnor-born Edwin Henry Lemare (1866-1934).

Newport had also marked the Golden Jubilee year by adding a spectacular clock tower to the right-hand side of the town hall façade. This splendid building, designed by John Nash (1752-1835), has a tetrastyle portico with Ionic columns on the first floor supporting an entablature and a dentilled pediment.

Now, ten years later, a more important Jubilee demanded something at least as spectacular. Shanklin thought long and hard. Aware that many towns up and down the land were erecting Jubilee Clock towers, Shanklin inclined towards its own public timepiece. It had been widely reported that the Brighton's Golden Jubilee clock had cost a thousand guineas. Shanklin was not quite in the same league.

There was considerable debate as to where it should be erected. Because the town did not really have a centre or a town square, wherever it went it would only be seen by some of the population at any one time. In the end it was decided to put it on the Esplanade near the entrance to the pier. This might today seem a peculiar place to put what was obviously going to be an expensive feature until one realises that in those days few people carried pocket watches, the wrist watch was unheard of and time was relatively important to people who made a living on the beach by hiring out boats by the hour.

The *Isle of Wight Observer* for December 1898 reported: 'that the Clock Tower, which is to form the memorial of Her Majesty's Diamond Jubilee will shortly be erected on the Shanklin Esplanade, the tender of Mr White, a local builder, to do the work for £195 having been accepted by the District Council…'

It is not clear whether the sum of £195 was to cover building the tower and installing the clock, only building the tower, or merely fixing the clock into a suitable stone structure. The cost of even a small four-faced turret clock would have been in the region of 30 guineas (£31.10/-). Probably it was just the stonework for which he had tendered.

And so Mr John White of Weymouth Villa, Wilton Park Road, got the job of building the tower for the clock. The site selected was close to a public drinking-fountain and horse-trough where the horses that spent their working time shifting bathing machines in and out of the sea were led twice a day to take a drink.

The day of the actual Jubilee, Sunday, June 20th, 1897, came and went. Shanklin put its date for celebrations forward one year to 1898. The foundation stone for the clock tower was duly laid by Mrs Margaret White Popham on Wednesday April 3rd, 1899. Her husband, the much-loved Francis White Popham, Lord Mayor of Shanklin, had died in 1894. It was a further full year before the task was completed. The belated dedication of the completed clock and its formal starting took place on April 17th, 1900. Whoops!

Better late than never, this fine clock still stands on the Esplanade. It miraculously escaped damage in the bombing of the Second World War and, although neglected for the duration, it happily restarted and onece more chimed the hours and quarters into modern times. Early in the 21st century, the proprietor of the Osborne House, a hotel almost exactly opposite the Clock, applied to the council to have the Clock silenced as it kept his visitors awake at night.

A timorous council, incapable of standing up to such a blatantly stupid complaint, immediately had the Clock silenced. Shortly afterwards, the Osborne Hotel closed down.

Set into the stonework of the Jubilee Clock tower and positioned at a height to suit both young and old is this inscribed plaque. As a subscriber to the construction and erection of this showpiece, this is the very least which those people might expect. Which is why it is a pity that the piece wasn't completed until April 1900!

Queen Victoria's Jubilee Clock on Shanklin Esplanade started life as something of an afterthought. Having seen Newport's ceremonial clock grafted onto the side of the town hall ten years earlier, Shanklin felt it ought to do one better. It took a long while to bring to fruition and the foundation stone was not laid until April 3rd, 1899. It would be a further year before the task was finished. On April 17th, 1900, it was formally unveiled – three years after the Queen's actual Jubilee year. This picture shows the crockets and the spire surmounted by a weather-vane over the high chamber that housed the two-bell twin-hammered chime that marked the hours as shown on the four-faced clock. From top to bottom the Clock Tower stood 40 feet high. In 2012 a plaque was added to the tower to mark the Diamond Jubilee of Queen Elizabeth. Today it is a Grade II Listed structure. Pity the historic flagpole and yardarm, seen in the background, was not similarly respected: the local council cut it down in 2012.

People sometimes ask why the ceremonial clock was erected on the sea front instead of in the town itself. The answer is simple. There were no other clocks on the Esplanade and at that time few people carried pocket watches. Those who worked the bathing machines and others needed to know the time, especially those who hired out boats by the hour. A time indicator on the sea front was thus a blessing for many. This photo was taken after 1918: the ruins of the burned-out first pier pavilion can be seen in the background. The pierhead jetties have gone, removed in March, 1916.

The Town

At the end of the 18th century Shanklin had a population of just 100. Sandown was too small to get much of a notice and was described as 'the village by the sandy shore'. In 1851, according to Brannon, Shanklin comprised 78 houses and had a population of 355. By the time of the 1861 Census, the number of houses had risen to 104 and the population to 479. There were two hotels. Spin forward to 1891 and we find the number of people had increased to 2,369 described as 'fixed population' and excluding comparatively vast increases due to summertime visitors.

By 1906 the population had risen to about 4,533 and there were six churches – three Established and the others 'Free' churches. There were twelve hotels.

This last statistic indicates that holidaymakers and visitors had been coming to Shanklin for a very long time. And if Jane Austen, Longfellow and John Keats had their eyes on Shanklin as a relaxing destination then one can be pretty certain that by the end of the 18th century news of its attractions must have been in wide circulation.

To begin with, as we have seen Shanklin comprised a cluster of settlements with what we now call the Old Village as its nucleus. That there was a demand for accommodation quite early on is evidenced by the decision of William Williams to build his hotel in 1824. Interestingly, White's *Gazetteer* for 1859 lists this building as the Shanklin Hotel suggesting that it was the first such establishment. Although rebuilt and greatly enlarged, it is still there today, only now we call it Hollier's.

Indeed, this was the first hotel as distinct from boarding houses in the town. Of the handful of sea front cottages that existed in those days, at least one was rented out to visitors in the opening decades of the 19th century. An even bigger hotel was to follow and that was Jeremiah Rayner's. He leased it to John Dash in 1833. Dash was clearly a fellow who sought status amongst his fellow men for he considered that by adding a letter 'i' to his name he might pass for an aristocrat possibly with European origins. So he became 'Daish' and to this day we call it Daish's Hotel.

Quite early on, Shanklin became a sought-after venue by foreign dignitaries and aristocrats. While the Esplanade's Royal Spa Hotel, built in 1871-1872, would openly court such visitors, Europe's top people were no strangers to the narrow streets of Shanklin.

Richards, writing in 1914, asserts that the Island attracted more German visitors than any other either English or American destination and in turn quotes from the pen of Henry Hamilton Fyfe (1865-1951), the renowned one-time London newspaper journalist, who said:

> The Germans are drawn to the Isle of Wight by the same attractions which have made the Italian Riviera such a favourite German holiday-ground. There is here all the velvety enchantment, all the luxuriance, all the beauty of the Ligurian coast. The people have soft voices. The country has soft curves. After the harshness of the Prussian climate, after the sandy wastes which surround Berlin, this wooing atmosphere, these gently rolling downs, these flowery meadows, these woods washed almost by the murmuring sea, fill the Teutonic soul with content. The German, as Mr Price Collier [*Germany and the Germans, From an American Point of View*, New York, 1914] brilliantly contends in his latest book, is an idealist, a creature of sentiment. His nature is to dream,. It is only by forcing himself against his temperament that he becomes a 'hustler'. Therefore he enjoys the mildness which some Englishmen say is enervating.

Incidentally it was John Morgan Richards who, in September 1903, purchased Steephill Castle and its estate from Charles Mortimer.

The Island had much to offer, with attractions that ranged from sailing at Cowes to horse-racing at Ashey. The latter, which began on Whit Monday, June 1813 and continued until Whit Monday, June 1930, was closely followed by many in all walks of Island life. Shortly after the 1930 season closed, the grandstand burned down, marking the end of racing on the Island.

The Chine Inn is another ancient Shanklin building although it was almost completely destroyed by fire in 1869 and had to be rebuilt. On another occasion, the access road to the Inn collapsed, trapping people in the Inn for some while. The Chine Inn was run by another old Shanklin family – the Proutens.

Shanklin's real period of development began around 1865-1870 when much of the High Street and its surroundings were built. That this coincided with the opening of the railway line from Ryde was no casual coincidence. Along with shops came branches of the principal banks. Early closing day in Shanklin was Wednesdays at 1.00 pm.

With the Queen and Prince Albert at Osborne, it was not unknown for Shanklin to have the occasional Royal party on a sight-seeing tour drive through. Now that the Esplanade sported the Royal Spa Hotel and its owner, Archibald Hinton, openly courted the nobility and aristocracy from other countries in Europe, things began to change.

Shanklin clearly coveted the handle 'Spa' and while The Royal Spa Hotel's owner had gained his experience on the fringes of such establishments, he had to face the established competition of Brighton and Bath. Neither, though, combined the charm that was Shanklin's. True, Brighton had its Royal Pavilion and direct sailings to Dieppe and, true, Bath had ancient and strong connections to the Roman occupiers, but these could not really be given 'Spa' status. Shanklin, with its special waters and insular location, had gained a reputation for possessing a charm that one found nowhere else.

If Brighton became a popular spa for those British hypochondriacs that frequented crystal-gazers, palmists and all those sorts of mediums that thrive on naive beliefs, and despite Baedeker writing warmly about it and hotels, it never quite appealed to the aristocracy and nobility of Europe. On the other hand, Hinton's Royal Spa Hotel, isolated on the Isle of Wight accessed only by boat, clearly hit a correct note in those elevated places.

In the years to come, Shanklin became rather blasé over these sightseeing oligarchs and it became more and more common to see an expensive carriage and horses or, later, a motor car bearing upper-class visitors. That Shanklin saw to move with the times is demonstrated in its architecture. Buildings put up at this time often reflect an associated status that one might only find in Ryde and Newport.

One of the buildings that set out to impress was the Shanklin Institute opened in 1879. Possessed of a somewhat austere façade with a columned portico, five years later it was expanded to include a Reading Room and an amusement section with billiard tables. It was also the headquarters of the Shanklin Chess Club. In 1913 it also became Shanklin Town Hall but after a fire in 1925 there was a period of limbo during which the future of the building was the subject of debate. The denouement continued until August of 1932 when reconstruction began. The old building was partially demolished and reconstruction began the following year. On March 31st, 1934, the new structure opened as combined town hall and 700-seat theatre.

During the Second World War the building was used for dances and various other types of entertainment. Post war, it was to present many concerts and plays. In the 1950s, Ernest English presented his Sunday evening 'Music Is Fun' series introducing the music of Bach, Beethoven, Schubert and Wagner to summertime visitors. A decade later the same venue hosted the Midland Symphony Orchestra conducted by Victor Fleming (1901-1991) under the auspices of the IoW Subscription Concerts Society.

Going back to the 19th century, development on the East Cliff saw one built for Francis Pittis of Newport who was knighted in the year of the Queen's Jubilee and died in 1883. The second new house, Vernon Cottage, was for the barrister and artist Edward Vernon Utterson (1776-1856).

Further afield in about 1873 an unusual architectural gem was erected on Keats Green. The co-called Gentlemen's Club was quite unlike any other building in Shanklin or on the entire Island. Unfortunately, the Club did not last but Keats Inn, which followed it, did and continued well into the 21st century. Today this one-time public house and hotel is private flats. At least it has suffered minimal external alteration.

Well worthy of mention is the church of St Saviours on the Cliff. Serving an ecclesiastical parish formed in 1869, it is one of the few churches on the Island that possesses a peal of eight bells. Impressive and imposing, it dominates many pictures taken of the Esplanade and pier by virtue of its size and position. The body of the church was erected in 1869 but the handsome tower and spire was not completed until 18 years later.

There's an odd story about this handsome tower. It was built to the design of architect W O Milne. William Oswald Milne (1847-1927) had what he considered to be the clever idea of directing the smoke from the church's boilers so that it passed out through one of the four pinnacles. This was to prove a catastrophic design mistake, for the heat and smoke hastened the decay of the stonework. And the tower was built of local stone which was not of the best quality. The upshot was that these quickly began to deteriorate. Combined with the fact that the bells were hung too high and in a frame which threatened the stability of the spire itself, the bells had to be silenced.

And so it remained until a massive and expensive renovation in 1985 which saw the removal of the four pinnacles and the re-hanging of the restored bells.

A renowned and widely appreciated feature of the Keats Green clifftop walk has long been its flourishing and colourful profusion of hydrangeas that fringe the path at the cliff edge. These appear in many picture post cards and drew mention not only in town guides but independent reviews. The astute members of the Shanklin History Society have traced the history of this feature and uncovered quite a fascinating tale.

It all began in 1902 when at a Shanklin District Council meeting on September 2nd, a town councillor named William Holling proposed that the summit of the cliff from the Chine to Hope Road, about half a mile in length, be planted with hydrangeas: He spoke of the great luxuriance attained by this grand flowering shrub in Shanklin, owing to climate and soil, suggesting that it would make the town even more famous than at the present. After a debate the proposal was carried and the task for selecting suitable sites given to the Highways Committee.

Tenders for the supply of the hydrangeas were opened that October and it was agreed to purchase a quantity from Michael Spartali, the Greek Government consul who resided at Shanklin's Rylstone House and apparently had another home at Godshill to which was appended a large plant nursery. From here, Spartali advertised a wide range of trees, shrubs roses and chrysanthemums. His price for hydrangeas was £2 per hundred, delivery free, for the autumn planting season in 1902. Just how many hydrangeas were planted is not known but it certainly created a feature of great beauty that became a famed feature for many years to come.

The 1939-45 War found Shanklin on a flight-path for enemy bombers on their way to Southampton or Portsmouth. Often Shanklin was used as a target for spare or hitherto undischarged ordnance. Almost inevitably these were low-level attacks and thus the bombs were often travelling at a shallow angle rather than vertically. Some of the buildings in the town were struck by bombs that were travelling almost horizontally, passing through one building and exploding in the next.

Shoppers found themselves the target of low-level machine-gunning on several occasions and there were stories of women running for their lives in Regent Street as aircraft passed low overhead shooting up pedestrians on the pavements.

After the 1939-1945 War, Shanklin would struggle to return to even its between-wars status. Foreign travel and, in particular, air travel, had irrevocably altered the British holiday makers' approach to the seaside vacation. And Shanklin was on the slippery slope from which it would never recover.

A barometer of Shanklin's development is undoubtedly the Old Village, that surprisingly small cluster of very old buildings which centres on the Crab Inn, a 16th century building with strong connections to King Charles 1. This has been pictured by photographers throughout all the years of photography. Importantly (for the historian), these generations of cameramen have all stood at almost the same spot by the wall of Hollier's Hotel to get their pictures. There are thousands of these views, all similar save for the passage of time. I shall be showing you a number of these, each differs in some important way and represents the passage of time. Here is one of my earliest taken in about 1865 and showing a thatcher at work. His ladder in the roadway is unlikely to inconvenience anybody. The cottages on the left have large front gardens.

When Charles Wheatstone (1802-1875) invented stereoscopic photography in 1832 he unleashed a technology that would gain instant popularity and result in almost everything of interest being depicted in what we call today 3D. One of the earliest of these stereo images was of Shanklin Bazaar about 1855. Here is one of that pair of almost-matching photos revealing the Old Village cottage enjoying what today's young marketing analysts might describe as 'encouraging foot-fall.'

It is about 1860 in Shanklin. The Crab Inn in those days was just one building, the annex built to the right of the main cottage not erected yet. The thatch on the Crab's roof looks a little past its best. The dormer windows in these early pictures are straight-thatched: much later on they would be given 'eyelids'. It was a safe time to walk in the road and speeding horse traffic would have been a rare occurrence.

From 1876 this view of the Old Village shows that the foliage behind the Crab Inn has grown and the cottages on the left have lost some of their front gardens due to road-widening. Street lighting has appeared with a gas lantern on the corner of the left-hand cottages. The gas mantle would not be invented for another fifteen years so this was merely an open gas flame. The Library is housed in the first cottage on the right.

Here we see that the Crab Inn has had a major addition in the form of a gabled extension to the right of the old building. There is also a thatch-roofed gabled walkway from its front gate. These additions are thought to have been added in 1897 and were associated with the Diamond Jubilee year of Queen Victoria.

The Second World War drastically reduced the amount of normal maintenance that could be undertaken on non-military property and it was into this category that the Old Village fell. When this photograph was taken in September 1946 there was still much catching-up to be done. Unrenewed since pre-war, here's some rather time-expired thatch. The white line in the roadway is the only visible concession to modernity.

From an unusual viewpoint a pleasing result showing Vine Cottage photographed in September 1946. The thatcher's work has been battered by weather on the nearest corner and the decorative liggers and twisted spars have come adrift and are missing.

Into modern times and a picture taken in July 1947. Observe how the trees have grown behind the Crab Inn.

An early and perhaps unfamiliar view of the Old Village. This April 1866 image was taken from the end of the High Street with the Crab Inn just round the corner to the left. Immediately left is the doorway and workshop of the local saddler. On the right side is the shop of Samson the newsagent and stationers with the post office next door down the hill.

In this photograph dated October 11th 1925 is the upper part of Shanklin High Street looking up towards Martin's Library.

A view of the lower High Street in about 1905 showing the draper's store of John Bailey, right, and the lower portion of the United Reformed Church's tower, left. In the centre is a very early motor car. Bailey occupied this whole site and the sign on the extreme right-hand wall reads: 'Drapery Millinery Dressmaking Hosiery Gloves Etc Departments'. The dark disk-shaped sign on the shop fascia, right of centre, advises that the shop is also an AA (Automobile Association) Agent. John Bailey opened his store on this site in 1871 and expanded to the whole block. After 141 years the business closed in 2012.

Looking north down Shanklin High Street showing the imposing building erected for the Provincial Bank positioned to face up the street. Along with the Mall or raised pavement, right, it survives to this day. Just visible between the trees on the right and above the wall is the original squat spire on the tower of the United Reformed Church further down the hill. On the left is William Thomas Deek's Chemist shop. The protruding sign over the door gives Deek's name with the addition of the line 'Manufacturers of High Class Aerated Mineral Waters'. The picture dates from 1905.

Facing page upper: When the United Reformed Church was built in the lower High Street in 1883 the four-tier tower included a short and squat Tuscan-style spire as seen here. Prominent in this view of the lower High Street is the corner building of the Provincial Bank of England, in itself imposing and architecturally pleasing. The church tower would suffer lasting damage in the bombing of Shanklin town and have to be rebuilt in the 1950s.

Facing page lower: A similar view from 1909 shows a busy street scene with pedestrians sharing the roadway with horse-drawn traffic.

The Town

Facing page upper: Back in the days when there was less traffic pollution as well as scant knowledge about airborne contamination, butcher's shops across the land looked like this one. Here we see the carcass-bedecked frontage of Thomas Knighton's Shanklin High Street shop. The picture dates from around 1905.

Facing page lower: A view of Shanklin High Street showing Martin's Library – the shop with the awning at the right. William Beavan Martin set up business in close-by Sandown around 1878, opening his Shanklin branch in 1886. Besides some 4,000 books all on public lending, he also carried most of the top-selling periodicals of the time. As well as books, Martin was also a musical instrument dealer advertising the best in pianofortes, American (reed) organs, violins &c, not to mention sheet music. But Martin is remembered for another unrelated innovation – he was the first to introduce early closing day to the area. The shop shut at 1.30pm on Wednesdays. Soon other retailers would follow his lead and in 1911 his bold move would become a part of the Shops Act. In this picture, the two-part overhanging sign also advertises picture postcards. Notice the fine brickwork on the tall, exposed gable wall. The small isolated shop in the middle is a former chocolate shop advertising Cadbury's and Fry's sweetmeats. Visible in the narrow centre window is a SOLD poster indicating that the premises had just changed hands. Nearest the camera, left, is another empty shop with estate agents and auctioneers Wallis, Riddett & Co's notice board on the wall outside. This is flanked by two identical posters advertising Greenham & Co, 'the Local Wine Merchants'. The picture was taken on October 11th, 1929.

A busy day in the High Street with the Midland Bank on the left and the raised pavement of the Mall on the right. Of course, the picture might just have been taken on a Wednesday afternoon for this was Early Closing Day for Shanklin. Following the introduction of the principle of Early Closing by Martin's Bookshop, all shop staff now had a half-day mid-week break. This was one of the provisions of the 1911 Shops Act. Towns could set to which day of the week the Act would be applied – invariably Wednesday or Thursday – and this date would be published in all guidebooks for the benefit of travellers. Introduced as part of the Liberal welfare reforms of 1906–1914: the Act was repealed in 1994.

During the bombing the tower of the United Reformed Church suffered extensive blast damage. In 1946, extensive cracking was discovered so the decision was taken to demolish it. The opportunity was taken to rebuild the tower in a slightly more modern style while retaining the dominant features. Work started in June 1952 and a foundation stone was laid the following year. Completed in 1954 it blends well with its surroundings. While there is no spire, the corner pinnacles serve to retain a pleasing balance – a feature lost to today's modern architects. Left in the picture we find the bank building now renamed the National Provincial.

Another High Street view, this one taken from further up the street looking backwards at Martin's Library. The shopfront, just visible above the awning, reads 'Bookseller W H Martin'. Founder W B Martin died in 1900 but his enterprise was continued by Wavell Henry Martin. Another photograph from October 11th, 1929.

Thomas Crone was in business in furnishing and upholstery at 17, High Street. Here he poses for the photographer just before the outbreak of the First World War. He appears to have had a sideline in hiring bath-chairs for the elderly and push-chairs for the youngsters. The seat of the lengthy three-wheeler parked in the roadway carries a notice reading 'For Hire' on it. The large number of books shelved in the window behind him might suggest yet another activity. His father had been a noted local cabinetmaker.

A quiet corner in Steephill Road in 1932 as a local bus gets a polish in its garage. The cream K3 telephone kiosk is a rarity. Designed in 1929 by Sir Giles Gilbert Scott, the vast majority of these 'phone boxes were in red-painted metal: this is cream-coloured concrete and reckoned at the time to be a cheaper version. Examples survived into the late 1930s.

A photograph dated September 3rd, 1900, looks down the High Street from the start of the Mall, right. Shanklin Cycle Depot, left, is two doors up from Nicholls Portrait Centre where commercial photographs and *cartes de visite* were available.

This rather quaint pair of cottages once stood in the High Street opposite the junction with tree-lined Regent Street. Seen here in May of 1932, they were swept away to create a site for the erection of the 850-seat Regal Cinema. This would not be Shanklin's first cinema for that had been the Playhouse in Palmerston Road which was built 'on the cheap' by a local trader using steel girders salvaged from the recently burned-down pier pavilion. This 450-seat cinema opened in 1920 and underwent some modernisation in June 1939 when the BTH sound system from the Regal Cinema was installed. By then the cinema had been sold and was operated by the Playhouse (Shanklin) Ltd who also operated the nearby Regal Cinema built on the site seen here. The old Playhouse was shut throughout most of the war and afterwards opened as a summer-season-only cinema until the late-1950s. In 1962 it was converted into an independent bingo club and this ran until 1995 when it closed for good, being demolished in February 2010, the site being used for flats.

Designed in the then-popular art deco style and built by Playhouse (Shanklin) Ltd, the Regal opened on August 22nd, 1932. As cinema entertainment changed and venues from the between-wars years had to be expensively upgraded, by 1965 the owners of cinemas nationwide sought to off-load their now-burdensome investments. In October that year, the Regal was leased to Star Cinemas Associated Holdings of Leeds. In due course this firm was absorbed by Cannon Group which took over Star in the 1980s. Re-named the Cannon Cinema, it finally closed its doors on October 3rd, 1986. While preserving the external profile of the façade, the building has now been converted into apartments and offices. The original cinema double entrance doors have been retained. Interestingly, the building next door still stands. Funnily enough, as a building, the old Playhouse which preceded it lasted that little bit longer before vanishing completely.

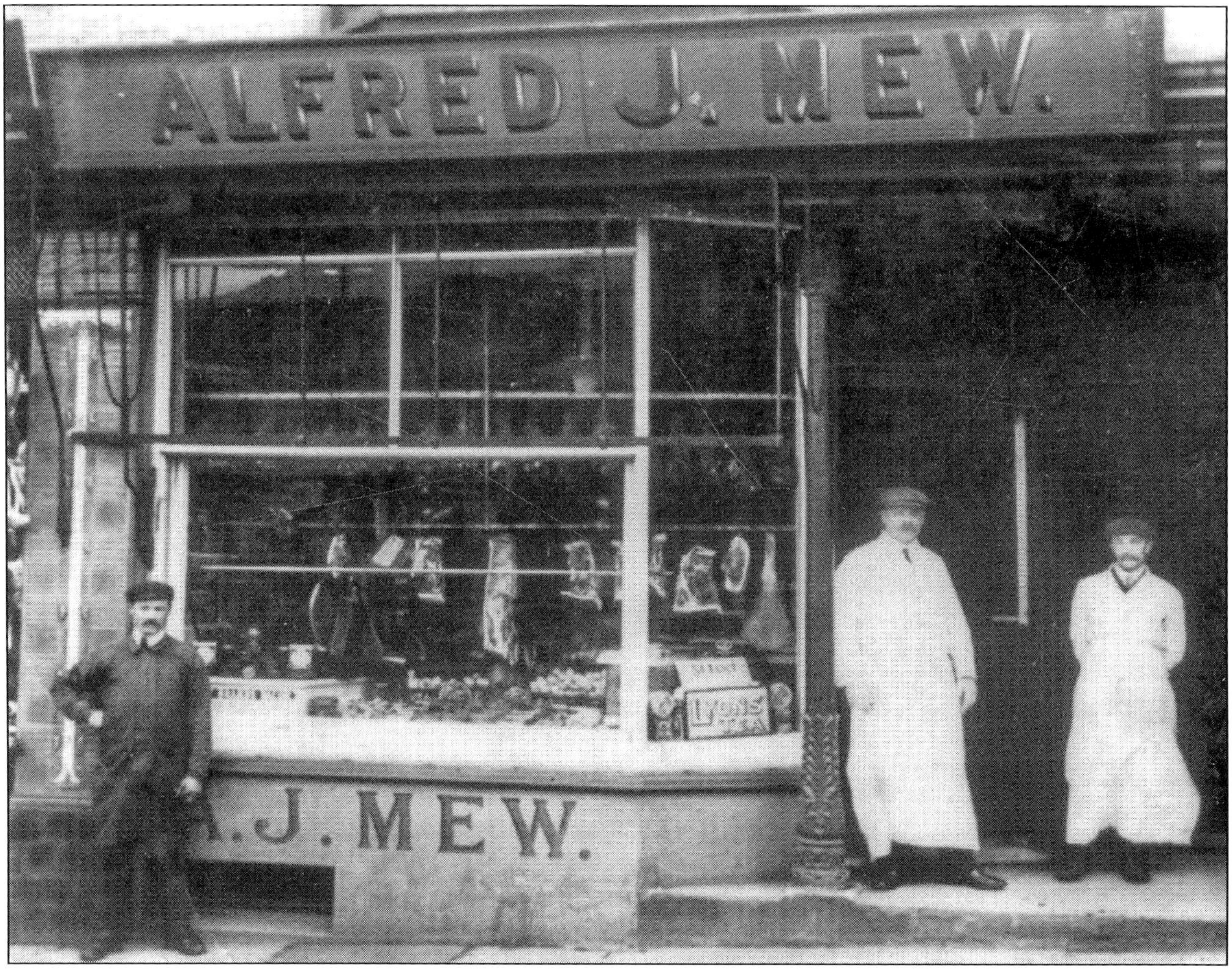
ALFRED J. MEW.
A. J. MEW.
LYONS

Excellence combined with Economy
Timothy Whites.
THE Reliable HOUSEHOLD STORES.
Timothy White Co Ltd
TIMOTHY WHITES
HOUSEHOLD STORES

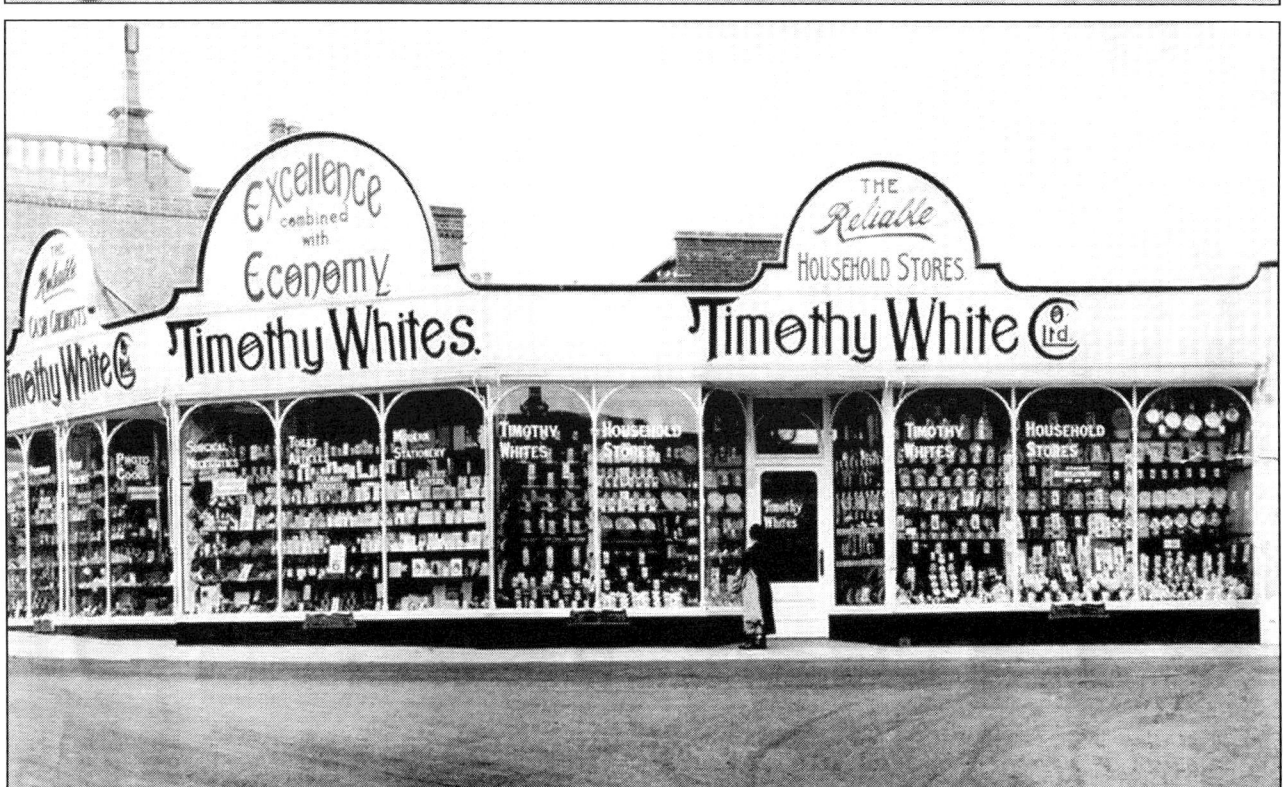

Facing page upper: Alfred J Mew's butcher's shop in the High Street seen around the year 1888. This illustrates very well both the shopkeepers' pride in their trade, plus the style of dress of the time. The moustache and cloth cap were de rigeur. In the narrow angled window, centre, is a notice advertising Lyon's Tea.

Facing page lower: Timothy Whites was once a fixture in almost every high street in the land. Latterly remembered as dispensing chemists and rivals to Boots, the business had an unusual beginning. Founder Timothy White began in 1848 as a ships' chandler in Portsmouth. Determined to better himself, he qualified as a pharmacist in 1869 and opened his first retail outlet. By 1890 he was one of only four UK pharmacists to have more than ten branches, mostly in southern England. As was fairly normal practice at that time, besides being retail chemists his shops also carried hardware and his rapid expansion led to the establishment of Timothy Whites Ltd in 1904. In 1935 the concern merged with Taylors Drug Co Ltd creating Timothy Whites & Taylors. Number 1 Shanklin High Street and 2 Regent Street represented these corner premises opposite the newly-opened Regal Cinema in this 1933 photograph. Post-war, the business was almost exclusively known as plain Timothy Whites but in 1968 the enterprise, which had a total of 614 shops nationwide and a combined turnover estimated at £33m, was sold to Boots Pure Drug Co. The Timothy Whites name disappeared in 1985 and this building is today branded Boots the Chemist.

Road accidents are nothing new and here a traction engine drawing the Victorian version of a skip loaded with rubble has lost control in the High Street, colliding with the railings and wall forming the raised pavement known as the Mall. On the side of the skip is painted 'Childs', the contractor's name. A crowd of young, mostly male, rubberneckers stands in the roadway behind. A curiosity in the foreground is a pair of well-adzed put-logs lying on the pavement. The purpose they served is unknown.

This view from October 11th, 1929 looks down towards the Provincial Bank building on the corner ahead. Besides advertising sporting equipment for tennis, protruding shop banners on the left side of the street advise us of a china and glass retailer, a chemist, and one that reads 'This is Holden's'. Holden Brothers were motor engineers.

Shanklin's Regent Street was lined on both sides with trees which grew until they overhung the roadway. They survived into the 1960s when they were cut down. In the centre of this summer 1936 view is the newly-opened store of F W Woolworth. This extensive chain of shops developed its sites in most towns in Britain and here the new building is of red brick tastefully arranged in the Georgian style. This memorable department store, which played a part in many people's lives, survived until 2008 when, after a chapter of takeovers and ownership changes, the entire chain spectacularly collapsed and the name was gone for good from UK high streets. The site was formerly the offices of the local paper, *The Guardian*, pulled down in April 1936.

Hollier's was originally known as Williams' Hotel. Here is an advertising card dated 1837 showing an engraving of the building. Built in 1824 by William Williams with a thatched roof, it passed into the Hollier family which originated in Niton via William and Alice Hollier. They died in 1875 and 1879 respectively. Henceforth it was known as Hollier's. Around 1880 it was rebuilt to a larger size and at the end of the 19th century the proprietor was Eugene Schmitt, a former Margate hotelier.

Hollier's Hotel in the Old Village back in the days when it had a thatched roof. On the left is the doorway to A J Walker's newsagent and novelty shop with a good display of stereo images down the side of the doorway. The photograph is dated August 1865. The proliferation of ivy on walls and buildings confirms that this type of infestation must have been welcomed in the widespread but completely misguided belief that it offered some sort of added protection to the stonework. In fact, it is now understood that ivy penetrates walls and allows moisture through.

Hollier's Hotel pictured about 1880. Some of the ivy has gone but the chimneys are well covered. Right is Buckell's Tearooms and Garden Warerooms with a lamp-standard on the corner in what today would be classified as a vulnerable position.

Most of the pictures of the Old Village are taken where the photographer has stood with his back to Hollier's Hotel. In this view from outside the Crab Inn, the photographer looks back up the hill to view the ivy-clad façade of Hollier's. The prominent noticeboard right on the corner reads 'Apartments Luncheons Dinners and Teas'. The lamp standard has been replaced by a bracketed lamp from the corner wall of the cottage.

In this 1936 photograph we see a couple playing clock golf on the finely-manicured lawn in the hotel grounds while staff serve refreshments to other guests in the garden. When the game of 'clock golf' was introduced at the end of the 19th century, Hollier's was one of the first to set out a 'course' in its grounds.

Hollier's was the first real hotel as distinct from those places that offered lodgings. Soon afterwards came a second and here is one of George Brannon's engravings of about 1861 showing 'Daish's Family Hotel and Boarding House'. This promotional advertisement says 'Commanding Extensive Views of the Sea'. The hotel remains today exactly where it was in the mid-19th century and views of the sea remain few and far between. Perhaps the art of truth-bending is older than we might think?

Built soon after William's Hotel (Hollier's), what became known as Daish's Hotel was built by Jeremiah Rayner and leased to John Dash (1802-1883) in 1833. Dash went and changed his name to 'Daish' around 1820. One supposes that he considered it gave his Island roots more of a Continental flavour. He certainly appears to have catered for the upper-class of holidaymaker. Viewed from the gardens this prospect of his establishment gives an indication of the style and comfort available to guests in the mid-1880s.

Now described as Daish's Family Hotel, this view dates from the very early days of the 20th century and shows the garden prospect, left. The building would be systematically extended over the years.

After the Royal Spa on the Esplanade, the second most influential hotel in Shanklin was Daish's at the top of the High Street by the Old Village. Significantly, today it is a Grade II Listed building. The hotel maintained a stable of coach horses and took its guests on tour round the Island in specially-built tiered coaches. Each party would be posed for the hotel photographer who would reckon to sell at least one postcard-sized print of his picture to each of the guests on the coach. Quite a promising investment in one glass photographic plate! Here a group poses for just such a photo-call. All of the guests including the children, are decked out in their best clothes and all save one lady wears a hat. The passengers at the rear of the coach are seated rather high for the Island's narrow and hilly roads. Note the pose of the groom with the leading horse.

It seems likely that Jeremiah Rayner erected the hotel as a speculative enterprise, leasing it to John Dash (Daish) very soon afterwards. Dash was an interesting character and in the year he took over (1833) he was listed as an innkeeper at Newport. Initially he seems to have managed to get up the noses of the Hollier's at the one-time William's Hotel, but this feuding seems to have faded by the 1860s. This photograph taken in the early 20th century shows the widened part of the road which provided a layby for the proprietor to park his coaches. The hotel was at this time a very high class establishment and kept a fleet of horse-drawn carriages for its guests. Note how the garden side of the building has been expanded.

The Roman Catholic Church of the Sacred Heart stands in Atherley Road. Built in 1906-1907, like the United Reformed Church in the High Street it had a small, squat spire atop a three-storey rectangular-sectioned tower. On January 3rd, 1943, it received a direct hit from a German bomb and the building suffered severe damage, reducing the tower to a single-storey ruin. It was rebuilt during 1956-1957 to a modern design preserving the surviving bottom portion of the tower and church entrance but creating a plain brick tower above with a large dominant central clock. The unadorned tower is in stark contrast to the pleasingly busy façade of the original seen here in about 1932. The house on the right, incidentally, survived the bombing almost unscathed and still stands.

Sibden Road was one of the main access roads into the village. To honour Queen Victoria's Jubilee in 1897 it was re-named Victoria Avenue. A pleasant, tree-lined approach down from the surrounding high ground, this remains an attractive road even if most of the trees have now followed those in Shanklin's Regent Street into oblivion. The author has fond memories of this road from distant 1937. Riding down here in an open-topped coach, a burst water-main on the left side of the road was sending a cascade of water in an arc across the roadway. The bus driver drew up short of this and asked the passengers what they would like to do – get out and walk round on the dry side of the pavement, or chance a fast ride through the wet. It was a hot day, the unanimous verdict was to carry on through. Yes, we got a bit wet, but it was a pleasure in that summertime heat and we soon dried out. Almost all of these trees matured into large specimens that stood until the 1987 hurricane which altered the prospect forever.

The Brunswick Hotel which stands high on Keats Green. The main subject here, though, is not so much the handsome hotel as the spire of St Saviour's Church. This image, from a picture postcard postmarked 1965, shows the church with its four pinnacles surrounding the base of the spire. In the major renovation of 1985, these were removed on the grounds that they were destabilising the actual spire.
At the same time, the bells were renovated and re-hung so that they could be rung for the first time in many years.

The building known as St Anthony's Convent of Mercy, Bella Vista, stood in Shanklin's Beatrice Avenue. Founded in 1898, it was run by the Sisters of Mercy who established a school in the town and went on to teach in others across the Island. In 2012 it was revealed that the last two remaining nuns had lived here for 56 years but a decline in numbers saw the pair move to another convent in Worthing. Plans to redevelop the building are currently in hand. The house, quirky in appearance, has quite a history. It was built around 1848 for Robert H Brannon, grandson of engraver George Brannon. His daughter Gertrude Mabel Brannon lived at Bella Vista until her death after which it became the Convent.

Off Popham Road, Rylstone House, today's Rylstone Manor Hotel, stands in extensive gardens which have been a public park since about 1914. This architecturally-interesting house has a rich past and a strong connection to the art world. It was built in 1863 and was offered for lease the following year. William Walker was the first lessee but two years later the occupier was Michael Spartali (1818-1914), the first Greek Consul to London. Establishing that Consuls exchange more

than just visiting cards, Spartali later rented Rylstone as a holiday home for the US Consul to London, one Edward Everett (1794-1865). Spartali's elder daughter Marie (1844-1927) was a talented artist who studied in London with Ford Madox Brown. She sat for Dante Gabrielle Rossetti, married the great Ruskin supporter, American-born William J Stillman, made a once-great name for herself as a portrait artist in the style fostered by William Morris and Rossetti, and exhibited at both the Grosvenor Gallery in London and Watts Gallery in Compton, Surrey. Marie Spartali-Stillman spent much time at her parent's home, Rylstone. Her mother died in 1913, a year before her father. Marie, long dismissed by the notoriously fickle art world as an 'amateur', is sadly forgotten today. Her parents' house at Shanklin stayed in private hands until about 1923 when the building was taken over by Harry Gray as a board residence.

Rylstone House after it was converted from diplomatic residence to private hotel in 1923. Constructed as a 'gentleman's home' in 1863, it is essentially the epitome of Victorian ornate architecture with an occasional nod to the Gothic, Tudor and Georgian styles. Built of stone, it features a jettied half-timbered upper storey with large projecting glazed upper bay windows and narrow divided chimney stacks built of sculptured bricks. Along with most other large houses, between 1939 and 1945, it was requisitioned for defence purposes. In post-war years it returned to private hotel status. Within its grounds stands an ornate wooden structure, Rylstone Chalet, erected in 1886. During the mid-'thirties this housed a museum devoted to stuffed Island birds and butterflies. Opened on April 17th, 1935, by the leading animal biologist of his era, Sir Edward Bagnall Poulton (1856-1943), the museum did not survive the war years. The Chalet is today the home of the Shanklin Town Band.

Rylstone's surrounding woodland had quietly embraced the house by the time this photograph was taken on September 22, 1937.

After the lessee, Spartali and his wife, moved out, eventually the spacious Rylstone Gardens was sold to the council along with Rylstone House which would be converted into a hotel. This picture postcard was issued during the first year of town ownership – 1923. With the advantage of being right on the clifftop as well as next to the Chine and Old Village, these gardens were an immediate attraction for visitors and residents alike. Access to the beach was via the Appley Steps which wove a tortuous course diagonally down the almost vertical cliff face. Sometimes you got to the bottom to find that a storm tide had carried away the last few steps.

Of all Shanklin's churches, St Blasius is by far the oldest and its origins are mediaeval. It is said to have been built during the reign of King Stephen which means between 1135 and 1154. Originally a mere rectangular chapel, in 1852 transepts were added and the building enlarged. Heavily restored in 1859, it has been said that all its original beauty was removed at that time. This is not entirely true and the church remains both beautiful and eccentric; its now-central bell turret meaning that the bell-ringers stand in the nave to be in full view of the congregation. Known colloquially as Shanklin Old Church, it is at the Wroxall end of today's town as Shanklin has spread northwards towards Brading. The church possesses a very fine pipe organ erected in 1874 by Forster & Andrews and today considered one of the best examples of their work. This photo was taken in 1882.

A unique feature of St Blasius is its substantial lychgate for this contains within its pitched roof a clock complete with bell. It was erected as a memorial to the Lord of the Manor, Francis White Popham (1829-1894) who held office as Lord Mayor of Shanklin for no fewer than 40 years. This is the only known example in Britain of a lychgate with a striking clock. There are also two well-carved oak gates.

Close to St Blasius is the Manor House Pond. This featured an unusual boundary fence which traversed the water from one side to the other.

A long, narrow strip of the south of the Island is unstable due to, among other things, layers of 'blue slipper' between layers of rock. Every once in a while there is movement. Usually this is relatively small and contained. In the historic past, however, the famous 'Landslip' was created along the whole of the Shanklin - Ventnor - Niton - Blackgang region. Today the origins of the famous Landslip are forgotten since it happened so long ago. It just happens to be a very nice place to visit and stroll through. This is one of the walks through this ancient event. It hasn't shifted any further for a long while, at least we hope not!

Luccombe Village

Three-quarters of a mile south of the Old Village is the small hamlet of Luccombe at Luccombe Down This was mere farmland and grazing for sheep until the early part of the 20th century when a few entrepreneurs built their houses upon these steep slopes. The advantages were impressive. Fine, unspoiled views out over the sea, Sandown Bay and Shanklin in total. More a cluster of homesteads than fully-fledged village, its major period of development was between 1927 and 1936. Long considered part of Shanklin, it stands high above the area that forms the easterly end of The Undercliff – that long, narrow stretch of heavily-wooded land that somewhere in ancient times, had slid downward forming a shelf at the bottom of a sharp escarpment.

Just south beyond the old centre of Luccombe village lies Luccombe Chine, accessible by a convoluted footpath. This geological feature is a wooded ravine, one of a small group of chines on the south east of the Island. Along with such features at Shanklin and Blackgang, Luccombe Chine was created by water erosion of the soft Cretaceous rocks. Eighty years ago, there was a settlement on the shore at Luccombe comprising five families plus a church and a chapel – all gone now.

As regards administration, although on hilly ground that overlooked Sandown Bay, just as close-by Shanklin was at one time under the jurisdiction of distant Brading, so Luccombe was officially grafted elsewhere.

A shift of emphasis came in 1933 when Shanklin Council merged with Sandown to form one administrative area. At the same time the hamlet of Luccombe came officially within Shanklin's jurisdiction. Previously it had been in the rural area linked to Bonchurch which was more Ventnor than the purvue of Shanklin.

Luccombe itself seemed geologically far removed from those turbulent times of distant past when The Undercliff was formed not too far away. That times of such turbulent terrain might return to influence such pastoral life seemed no more than an unlikely bad dream until one day in February 1910 when a huge section of the high ground simply came loose and slid down towards the sea. This swept away the small fishing community which resided at the foot of Luccombe Chine.

Considered, hopefully, an isolated event, this was soon forgotten and the pre-war development evolved. The small coterie that lived there were simply unaware of the fact that their homes were built on geologically unstable ground and that there had long been slight ground movements. After all, the view was just so outstanding…

In 1950, though, things changed rapidly and, after a period of heavy rain, the ground suddenly began to move. The days of this tiny hamlet with its carved wooden village name-board, post-box and bus stop (for it was served by a small bus operated by Bartlett's Garage in Sandown that ran from Shanklin Pier up the steep hill road and back again) were numbered.

Houses were literally pulled apart by the shifting earth as the narrow roadways tore asunder and, over the twenty years that followed, regular events systematically erased the old village. While new homes for Luccomites were later built further inland and on still higher ground, and although new paths were created through the shifting land as people continued to make their way down to the waterfront at Luccombe's own chine, all that was original was slowly destroyed. This event was recorded with some spectacular pictures as you shall see,

On March 4th, 1978, there came one of the worst landslides since the Blackgang Undercliff road in 1928 when a major part of the remaining Luccombe old village shifted. A 1,500-yard strip of land began moving at 6.30 pm on Friday March 3rd at the Bonchurch end and gradually spread northwards. By Saturday night, the Sandrock Spring, a large 5-bedroomed house, was gone. A house called Cliff View suddenly lived up to its name before disappearing 300ft down onto the beach. A nudist colony called the Southview Sun Club joined a caravan park and sports centre on the tumbling earth. Furniture and personal possessions joined in a slow tumbling mass to the rocks below.

The agile can still access the rocky shore down at Luccombe Chine, but the village of old is no more. And the one-time steps down to the shore have been lost to coastal erosion. For those who don't object to a bit of rock-scrabbling, the beach is just about an attainable goal. Getting back up may be another thing…

A short walk up the hill from Shanklin takes one to the hamlet of Luccombe. Today it is rebuilt further inland. Map from Sir Richard Worsley Isle of Wight, 1781.

The Luccombe area has always been extremely volatile and there are still occasional and, generally, less spectacular slips. An exceptionally large one took place in February 1910 when a huge section of Luccombe simply fell into the sea. This photograph shows what happened. Of course, it was soon forgotten and people began building on the slopes again. After all, the view was outstanding…

At the end of the pathway to Luccombe Chine was the final descent to the rocky beach below. This called for visitors to pass through a restriction probably intended to keep cows and cyclists from falling onto the stones below. A lovely picture looking inwards towards the high hills behind. As a child I played in this area while marvelling at the high-pitched twitterings of the skylarks above. Most people lose the ability to hear skylarks as they grow older. I have.

The track through the tiny settlement of Luccombe to the south of Shanklin Old Village in Georgian times was a delight with wonderful vistas at every turn. It skirted the village on the sea side and ended up as a meandering pathway past the oldest houses and the Hi-Da-Way Tearooms until eventually it dropped down to the beach at Luccombe Chine. This is how it appeared in 1937. The second half of the 20th century saw a cluster of extensive landslides through Luccombe which not only swept away the majority of the original village, but much of the scenic surroundings. There are still paths through Luccombe, but they are very different today. Unrecognisable, in fact.

Tucked away off the pathway seen in the previous view and just beyond the settlement of Luccombe Village was the Hi-Da-Way café and tea-rooms. Known locally as 'the shed in the trees' and seen here around 1930, this popular café advertised all the drinks of the period including Horlicks, Ovaltine, Bourn-Vita and Milk-Shakes while the noticeboard in the foreground offered the local Farmers' Ice Cream.

Hi-Da-Way extended the other side of the pathway to Luccombe Chine to what was called The Lawn where extra tables and chairs were set out to attract customers. It was a quiet and restful spot with the only sound being the endless singing of those skylarks above.

Luccombe centre was a smart well-manicured green bearing a decorated village name board, a brick-built letter box and a bus stop for W Bartlett's service back to Shanklin Esplanade. At the end of May, 1950, all this suddenly came to an abrupt end as the ground began to move. Buildings cracked apart and old Luccombe's tranquillity ceased. Here, what remains of the village centre has been fenced off. The house behind has lost an end wall. Soon the rest of the Luccombe of old would go, too. Eventually a new Luccombe village would materialise, but that would be built much further inland and away from the area at risk of movement. Or so it was planned… Since that wake-up call of 1950, there have been two further periods of extensive and destructive land movement, one in 1960-61 and another in 1987-88.

In pre-war days, Bartlett's local bus service ran from the Esplanade to the railway station, thence to the Old Village, Rylstone Gardens and then up to Luccombe Common with its access to The Landslip. It operated April to September. Occasionally passengers were asked to get out and push on the steep hills. After June 1950, when this major slip occurred, the houses on the right were effectively cut off. Those that had not fallen down were quickly demolished.

All of the homes to the left of this picture would either collapse over the next few days or would be peremptorily demolished to avoid unintentional injury or secondary damage. Luccombe Village was virtually obliterated in this natural event. People who lived there said that because they seemed so high up and far from the cliff edge they were safe from any earth slippage. They were wrong and lost their homes. Some of the affected houses were expensively designed and built: ground movement has no respect for such endeavours. The lady standing by the ravine in the roadway is June Windust, lending scale to the disaster.

The extent of the damage caused by this one event was as astonishing as it was extensive. Here is another part of the cliffside roadway through the town that cracked open and, over the days that followed, simply fell away into the sea below on the left. Right of centre can be seen a house which has just had its tiled roof removed as part of 'preventative demolition'. Those who were able to evacuate were faced with having to carry possessions a fair distance to the remaining stable bit of road back to Shanklin. Not so easy if you had a car in your garage.

One final photograph from that momentous occasion to emphasize the devastation to the roadway. Even those homes that escaped the first movement at the end of May and the start of June in 1950 were not safe. The houses seen here on the left would crumble away or be demolished over the weeks that followed. Luccombe was changed for good!

The Chine

What do we mean by chine? It is a word of Saxon origin and means a deep narrow coastal gorge, formed by water cutting through soft sandstone leading to the sea. There are no fewer than twenty chines on the Isle of Wight, to which fascinating folklore is attached because of their association with local smuggling, fishing and shipwrecks. Geologically, Shanklin Chine exists in Cretaceous rocks and gained fame during the Second World War for its involvement when it was used as training area for the 40 Royal Marine Commando battalion before the 1942 Dieppe Raid. It was also used to route one of the Operation PLUTO pipelines to France.

Shanklin's Chine has long been recognised as a beauty spot, rich in the flora that these sheltered and mineral-rich water-courses are famed for. It was created by a stream, which emerges high in the downs behind the town.

In the 18th century the Chine was an arduous climb for the intrepid. While it was a tiring struggle, it was used after dark by smugglers to get their spoil from the beach to places such as the back room of The Crab Inn where deals were done. In fact the Chine remained a vital link in the haven of smuggling that was 18th century Shanklin and it is reputed that a tunnel linked the upper part of the Chine with the Old Village. So prevalent was the passing of contraband via the Chine that Excise Officers were based in the Old Village until the Watch House near the Chine was built in 1820.

But in general those who were not being chased by Excise officers and who made it as far as the waterfall in daylight hours were impressed by its serenity and quiet beauty. There are signs that there were early efforts to open up the Chine and steps were provided at the shore end for the use of Excise officers on horseback in the execution of their attempt to stem smuggling.

In the very early 1800s the Chine was employed as a short-cut by a few enterprising matelots who had to get back to their ships in a hurry having spent too long in The Crab Inn's bar. Going downhill was one thing: getting back up was quite a different one. Jane Austen described it as a 'rough walk' and added that very few people managed to make it up to the waterfall at the top.

In 1817 the then Lady of the Manor authorised William Colenutt who lived in the Fisherman's Cottage at the beach mouth of the Chine to construct a proper pathway from shore to Old Village. Colenutt was a longshoreman with a subsidiary penchant for smuggling. He succeeded in carving out a series of pathways and bridges from the beach up to the Old Village which he then opened to the public. According to an 1882 guidebook, the charge for admission was 3d, later increased to 6d, a charge which prevailed until 1958.

The Chine was to become one of the first tourist attractions on the Isle of Wight, celebrating its 200th anniversary a few years back. Poet John Keats found inspiration for some of his greatest poetry while staying at Shanklin in 1819 writing that: 'The wondrous Chine here is a very great Lion; I wish I had as many guineas as there have been spy-glasses in it.' The Chine attracted all manner of visitors and proved to be a favourite subject for artists including Thomas Rowlandson and Samuel Howitt.

This attractive ravine soon became a 'must' on every Victorian itinerary, and there are numerous contemporary descriptions that contain phrases such as 'terrifically sublime' and 'savagely grand'.

During the Second World War the Chine was used for Commando training and many of its paths and bridges blown up or otherwise spoiled. While mentioning this, one might relate the sad tale of the great Chad's Rock which stood by the side of the Undercliff Road at Blackgang for centuries and appeared in many postcard views. This, it was said, was swept away when the 1928 landslide carried away the roadway. Not so. It was still standing in 1938 when I stood next to it. The Commandos from Shanklin Chine went to Ventnor in 1941 to examine the rock which subsequently they used in experiments to see how much explosive it would take to disintegrate it. This impressive landmark was thus needlessly destroyed as a 'training exercise' in time of war because 'it didn't matter'.

The subsequent involvement of the Chine with PLUTO (Pipe Line Under The Ocean) was merely another application that damaged the fragile beauty of the Chine in the years from 1939 to 1945.

When Peace returned to the Island, many things had to be put right that had been broken, damaged or destroyed. The Chine was one of them and this saw the construction of new pathways, steps and bridges using steel girders and metal planking. The upshot was a somewhat 'new look' Chine but, since there is no holding back Nature, quite quickly it returned to a serene beauty not far short of that which was forgotten.

Near the bottom of the Chine and not too far from the Fisherman's Cottage stands the so-called Honeymoon Cottage on an isolated ledge. This quiet and peaceful building, once a retreat for loving first-nighter couples, dates from around 1850. Today it is a gift shop and is said to have a resident poltergeist which quietly moves things around during the hours of darkness.

The Chine is in the private ownership of Anne Springman who succeeded to the property from her father. Born Anne Macpherson of Cluny, she was High Sheriff of the Isle of Wight 2002-2003 and received an MBE for her services to the Community in 2014. Her great-great uncle was Francis White Popham, the last Lord of the Manor.

Not quite the same today is this 1890s view of the Chine Road with its rich overhanging foliage. Only yards from the Old Village yet already in another world!

Chine Road in about 1909 showing a quiet and peaceful rural setting in an age when the road user was of equal importance to the pedestrian. A gas lamp casts a reassuring yellowish glow over the pathway for the after-dark walker.

At the top of the Chine, the stream flows across the road in a narrow open gulley. Smartened up over the years it remains a pleasing reminder that Nature got here first. This picture was taken in 1924 and shows the little footbridge to preserve the travellers' footwear and the long skirts of ladies. The watercourse flowed from right to left from whence it cascaded into the Chine as the famed waterfall. In a hot summer this was known to dry up and photographers, anxious to be seen to be earning their crust, would resort to 'picture retouching' to show a good flow.

By 1880, the Chine had been given a proper entrance with a gateway and fenced-off walkways. Fortunately we know exactly who took this photograph because his wetstamp appears on its back – H A Ives of Mayfield House, 3 Pier Street, Ventnor. He was also a bookbinder and newsagent. We will find another of his pictures further on.

The Chine has a long history since its first opening as a passageway to the shore. Photographed in 1882 and titled 'The Head of Shanklin Chine', its pathways were delineated by rough wooden fences and places where today's health & safety might raise eyebrows. A quiet and beautiful place to find peace and solace, it has always been renowned for its flora and fauna, much of which only grows in this sheltered area. The little waterfall emanates from a spring the other side of the access road beyond the woven wooden panel.

Below: A 1930s image of a tranquil walk through Shanklin Chine illustrating the quiet rustic pathways and a footbridge across the babbling brook fed from beyond the camera by the waterfall.

Depicted in 1903, the old stone bridge in the Chine has been a popular photographer's subject almost since the invention of the camera. This unusual, low view highlights the people seated on the parapet.

Ventnor photographer H A Ives also found this bridge fascinating and his picture, from a similar viewpoint twenty years earlier, suggests almost a totally different place – a clear demonstration of the fact noticed by the early explorers of Shanklin that there is always s fresh prospect in the Chine and things are destined never to stay the same.

This is what the entrance to the Chine looked like back in 1860 before it was landscaped for the public to visit. In the beginning it was considered a sort of 'emergency access' from shore to Old Village and reverse and mainly used by sailors and fishermen who came ashore in boats.

Two friends pause for a quiet smoke and a chat in the peaceful tranquillity of the Chine. The beauty of this natural cleft is revealed in this intimate photograph dated 1885.

Throughout history, the vast majority of visitors and holidaymakers to the Island arrived by sea. Only later did the convenience of air travel become available to those who could afford it and in the late 1930s the Island's four aerodromes – Cowes (Somerton), Ryde, Shanklin (Apse and, later, Lee) and Bembridge – saw regular services from London's Croydon and Heston Airports. Between the wars, paddle steamers plied the Solent. One long-time favourite was the *Lorna Doone*. Built on the Clyde in 1891, this 220-ft long 427 tonner worked for the niftily-named Southampton, Isle of Wight & South of England Royal Mail Steam Packet Company Limited, otherwise known as Red Funnel Steamers but colloquially as 'Fred Runnel Boats'. During both wars *Lorna Doone* was engaged in military work as a minesweeper. After the Second World War, her condition was deemed beyond repair and she was scrapped in 1948. The author travelled many times on this venerable old paddler as a small boy.

Another of the paddle-steamers was the *Whippingham*. Built at Govan, Glasgow, in 1930, the 825-ton 244-ft long vessel served with the Southern Railway on the Portsmouth-Ryde service. Impressed in time of war, like so many of these vessels, her first task was to take part in the Dunkirk evacuation between May 26th and June 4th, 1940. She only made one crossing but managed to save 2,700 troops. Later on she became a mine sweeper and later took on anti-aircraft duties taking part in the Normandy landings in June 1944. Once the war was over, it was back to the old Portsmouth-Ryde run but with the introduction of faster diesel boats, the steady, slow paddlers were called back into service less and less, usually only at the height of summer week ends to boost passenger capacity. After the 1962 season, she was withdrawn and went to the breakers-yard in Belgium the following May.

Horse-drawn public transport is of some antiquity but vehicle licensing did not begin until 1904 with the inauguration of motor-powered transportation. Not only were motor buses an innovation, but registrations were still a new thing. So it was when the Ryde-based Isle of Wight Express Motor Syndicate was established in 1905. Based at 80 Union Street, Ryde (later it moved to Pier Street), its formation on April 13th saw the arrival on the Island of its first motor bus – a 20 hp Milnes-Daimler double-decker with a Dodson body and marked DL 78. Capable of carrying 36 passengers, half inside and the other 18 on the open top with its wickerwork front, this vehicle ran between Ryde and Shanklin with a return fare of 1s 6d. Four buses were ordered for a projected service to all corners of the Island. It would be several months before the other three vehicles were delivered. It was not all plain sailing, however. The service began to experience problems during its first summer season. The buses proved to be under-powered and it was quickly decided to replace them. Services were suspended in October 1905 to enable alternative vehicles to be obtained. A much-reduced service, covering in the main only the east Wight and Shanklin, commenced in April 1906 using more powerful buses. At the end of the summer, a skeleton winter timetable was introduced. By the following March, the business was in trouble again and a further reduction in routes was made and fares were cut in a desperate attempt to survive.

The first motor bus on the Isle of Wight was Shanklin's link to the rest of the Island. Here we see DL 78 posing with a full load of passengers including two under the leather blanket next to the driver. The board below the windows of the lower deck reads 'Sandown & Carisbrooke'. The bus served a circular route starting from Ryde through Seaview, St Helens, Bembridge, Sandown, Shanklin, Godshill, Rookley, Carisbrooke, Newport, Wootton Bridge, Binstead and thence back to where it started in Ryde. These buses were withdrawn after little more than a year, as they were underpowered and thus performed below par on hills.

Here another of the motor buses is seen, this time DL 75 in Shanklin High Street with Prospect Road going off to the right. These vehicles could not tackle the steep hills to Ventnor and instead would have turned to the left of the picture and travelled to Rookley and thence Newport along the newly re-named Victoria Avenue. The services appear to have ceased in the summer of 1907. Although it was a short-lived enterprise, it pioneered an island-wide motor bus network. Its failure was in part due to over-ambitious plans to run routes all over the Island, not to mention the initial choice of unsatisfactory vehicles. On top of this there was local opposition, especially from the local well-established horse-drawn bus operators.

Soon there were numerous other Isle of Wight bus operators. One of them was Walkden's Garage based in Sandown. This business ran a shuttle service between Sandown and Shanklin with a mixture of vehicles among which DL 5585, pictured here, was a 1928 Morris Z fitted with the luxury of pneumatic tyres.

Important people visiting Shanklin were quite a common sight in the 19th and early 20th centuries. With the Royal Household at Osborne House plus the attraction of foreign dignitaries at the Royal Spa Hotel on the Esplanade, it was not uncommon to spot a prince or a duke – even an emperor – on your travels. Here people gather in the Old Village to see the Prince of Wales drive through Shanklin in his Rolls-Royce. The now-curious practice of hat-waving was the accepted method by which the nobodies greeted the somebodies.

A carload of high society parks outside Osborne & Sons, the High Street gentlemen's outfitters in Shanklin town. A sign outside advertises the one-time well-known brand of Aertex underwear. Aertex was a type of fabric introduced by a Manchester-based company in 1888. The work of a Lancashire mill owner named Lewis Haslam, it gained an immense popularity by virtue of trapping air between the warp and weft of the cloth to produce an insulating barrier between the warmth of the body and the atmospheric chill. Among the passing gawpers in this picture is a small boy, extreme right, who stands in his best suit and cap with a smart watch and chain in his waistcoat.

In 1866 the first steam train set off from Shanklin on its journey to Ventnor. Here it prepares to depart on its momentous journey. After dark, the guard would walk along the roofs of the passenger carriages, open the domed vents above each – and insert a pre-lit oil lamp to relieve the darkness within. This practice, widely enjoyed across the nation, was one reason why in a train crash so many involved fires where those trapped in the wreckage would be burned to death. Fortunately almost all Island rail accidents only involved low-speed shunting errors or derailments.

When the Ryde to Shanklin railway opened, there was still a need to transport people further on to Ventnor. The horse-drawn coaches that used to run direct from Ryde to Ventnor via Shanklin now continued their runs, this time starting from Shanklin Station. One of the coaches was somewhat prosaically called *The Rocket*. It is seen here in 1864 ready to take passengers from the steam train by the four-in-hand growler over the Downs to Ventnor.

Ventnor Station with the stationmaster proudly displaying the departure board revealing from whence trains leave for elsewhere on the line to distant (in Island terms) Ryde.

Shanklin railway station in the early 1900s with a train about to leave for Ventnor. The Ryde to Ventnor line was the first to open on the Island and the first through-train ran on September 16th, 1866, two years after the opening of Shanklin Station. The line was truncated at the time of the infamous 'Beeching axe' of 1966 and the track between Shanklin and Ventnor ripped up. There have been several notable plans to re-open it but it needs money plus the fact that the trackway on the other side of Landguard Manor Road – immediately behind the camera in this view – is now developed into a housing estate. And the brick bridge erected over Landguard Manor Road has long been pulled down. An old man named Bull who lived at 54 Green Lane remembered helping to build this when he was a boy.

Steaming its way into the history books, the last train pulls out of Shanklin Station to begin the long 294-feet climb on its way to Wroxall and finally Ventnor on April 18th, 1966. The Ryde-Ventnor line was then closed beyond Shanklin and the track bed mostly dug up and obliterated in an act created by the notorious Dr Beeching who savagely hacked Britain's rail system to pieces. The buildings on the left of the engine formed part of Shanklin's gas works which closed in 1957.

The church of St Saviour's on the Hill stands on the edge of Keats Green. Designed by architect Thomas Hellyer, construction of this dominant church began with the laying of the foundation stone in May of 1867. The bulk of the building was consecrated in May of 1869. In 1883 the vicar, the Rev Charles Burland, proclaimed that a spire was to be built to house a grand peal of eight bells. By 1887 the tower and spire were complete and some 75 cwt of bells cast and hung by Mears and Stainbank of London's Whitechapel Bell-foundry, makers of Big Ben. Sadly the bells were hung too high on a poorly-designed frame and by 1900 the tower was housed in scaffolding to enable repairs to be completed on cracked stonework. Bell-ringing was restricted due to increasing risks to the tower and then ceased for many years. By 1990 extensive repairs were needed to both tower and spire. At this time, the corner pinnacles of the spire were removed and the restored bells rehung so that they could be pealed. This view shows that the tower was effectively separated from the body of the church itself. One of the four pinnacles, dispensed with in that overhaul, had originally doubled as a chimney for the Church boiler creating unexpected structural mayhem. A Grade II Listed building, the clifftop church has been a dominant feature of many photographs taken on the seafront.

Cottage hospitals went out of fashion soon after the formation of the National Health Service in July 1948. At one time, Shanklin had three of them. These included the Home of Rest on Sandown Road and today called Winchester House, and the Cottage Hospital at the top end of Luccombe Road, which was the last to go. Created in 1947-1948, it conveniently burnt down prior to redevelopment. The author's first wife was a senior nurse there for some years. Third of the troika was this one in Landguard Manor Road. It was known both as Shanklin Cottage Hospital and the Arthur Webster Memorial Hospital. This was opened in 1905, a gift to the town by Richard Webster (Lord Chief Justice at the time, and later known as Lord Alverstone) in memory of his son Arthur who had died at the age of 28 after an operation for appendicitis.

Shanklin's Home of Rest stood at Lake, between Sandown and Shanklin and, while heavily revamped, is today known as YMCA's Winchester House. Originally it was associated with the Girls' Friendly Society offering affordable holiday accommodation for working women such as domestic servants, teachers, nurses, clerks, students, and factory workers. It opened in 1893 and its patrons were Princess Henry of Battenberg and The Bishop of Winchester. Here is a view of the building soon after it first opened showing the Chapel.

Published in *The Illustrated London News* for September 7th, 1946, this aerial view of Shanklin dates from that summer and reveals the extent of the bomb damage to the Esplanade at the end of the Second World War. Almost every building left of the pier has been badly damaged or destroyed. The Royal Spa remains intact and, at the extreme lower right, can be seen the narrow bridge used to transport PLUTO across the unwisely blown-up section of the pier. The Church of St Saviours and its dominant spire are clearly seen left of centre.

Timeline

RAILWAY
    Ryde to Shanklin: station opened   August 23rd, 1864
    Shanklin to Ventnor via Wroxall opened   September 10th, 1866
    Line closed from Shanklin to Ventnor   April 18th, 1966
    Last steam-powered train   December 31st, 1966
    First all-electric train Ryde to Shanklin   March 19th, 1967

ESPLANADE DEVELOPMENT
    Begun   1869

ROYAL SPA HOTEL
    First built   1872
    Four-gabled glass conservatory added   1880
    Hotel closed for 1939-45 War   August 1939
    Hotel demolished   1954-55

NEWNES' HYDRAULIC LIFT
    First built and opened   1891
    Demolished   1957
    Replaced by Concrete Monolith   1958

PIER
    Construction began   August 1888
    Opened at cost of £24,000   August 18th, 1890
    1st Pavilion opened   July 28th 1909
    1st Pavilion destroyed by fire   June 29th, 1918
    Pierhead landing stages removed   March 1916
    Pierhead landing stages replaced   May 1931
    2nd Pavilion opened   June 4th, 1927
    Pier cut in National Defence   1941
    Pier halves united (in stages)   from 1948
    Pier destroyed by gale   October 15th- 16th, 1987
    Remains of pier removed   1993

FLAGPOLE
    First erected in hotel front garden   pre-1880
    Moved across Esplanade to pier entrance   1890
    Cut down by council vandals   2012

ESPLANADE CLOCK (Queen Victoria's Jubilee)
    Foundation stone laid   April 3rd, 1899
    Inaugurated   April 17th, 1900
    Striking/chiming mechanism disabled   c.2010

EFFLUENT TANK BUILT ON ESPLANADE
    Tank installed and put into use   1928-29

CHINE
    Opened to public   pre-1813
    Damaged by Royal Engineers   c.1941
    Restored and re-opened   1946

St. SAVIOURS CHURCH
    Body of Church constructed   1869
    Spire completed   1887
    Side pinnacles removed   1985

Index

IFC – inside front cover.   IBC – inside back cover.

A

Adams, William Henry Davenport, author quoted   5
Aerodromes, the Island's four   84
Aertex underwear   88
Aircraft hangar, Bembridge converted to Shanklin theatre   7, 12
Aix la Chapelle, comparison   17
Albert, Prince   16, 40, 42
Alverstone   6
Anerley Gardens, London venue   16
Appley Steps   14, 35, 69
Apse Heath, Shanklin Aerodrome   3, 84
Arthur Webster Memorial Hospital   91
Asher, Capt Andrew   2
Ashey, horse-racing at   42
Askey, Arthur, comedian   7, 26
Atherley Road   66
Austen, Jane, novelist quoted   4, 42, 78
Automobile Association (AA)   21, 49
Auxiliary Fire Service   7

B

Babbacombe/Oddicombe Cliff Railway   36
Baedeker writes warmly re Brighton   43
Bailey, John, draper's store   49
Barney's Emporium   26
Bartlett's Bus Service, W, garage   72, 75, 76
Bath, spa town of   42
Bathchair hiring   55
Bathing machines, winter parking   6, 11, 12
Baths, relaxing chalybeate at Royal Spa   16
Bay Tree Cottage, Sandown Road   7
Bazaar, Shanklin   45
Beach Cottage   6
Beach defences, wartime   26
Beatrice Avenue   67
Beecham, Sir Thomas, conductor   17
Beeching, Dr Richard, his railway 'axe'   90
Bella Vista, convent   67
Bell-founders Mears & Stainbank   91
Bells, rung from centre of Church congregation   5, 70; church with peal of eight   43, 91
Bembridge, RNAS aircraft hangar converted to Shanklin theatre   7, 12; Aerodrome   84
Bennett, 'Bunny', Pier impresario   25
Bishop of Winchester   92
Black, Adam and Charles, publishers   5
Blackgang underdcliff road, great landslip of 1928   72
Blasius, St, church of   5, 70; its notable pipe organ   70
Bless 'em All, song   12
Blew, Ted, longshoreman   20
Blew's Bathing & Boating Office   20
Blue slipper clay   5, 35, 71
Board of Trade order for Pier   25
Bombing, World War 11   44; Shanklin's first   7
Bonchurch   5, 72
Booth, Webster, singer   7
Boots Pure Drug Co   59; Boots the Chemist   59
Bournemouth   28, 29
Bowling green, Shanklin   7, 12
Box Brownie camera   IFC, 2
Brading   4, 70
Brannon, George, engraver   5, 8, 42, 63, 67
Brannon, Robert H   67
Brighton   42, 43; Volk's Electric Railway   36; Victoria's Golden Jubilee Clock   40; Royal Pavilion   42
Britten-Norman Ltd, aircraft manufacturers   2
Brown, Ford Madox, artist   68
Brown's Golf Course, Sandown, PLUTO base   26, 32
Brunswick Hotel   67
BTH cinema sound system   57
Buckley's Tearooms & Garden Warerooms   62
Burland, Rev Charles, St Saviour's   91
Burlesques, The, Pier opening show   25
Bus, the first petrol-driven on the Island   85; Walkden's Garage   87; Bartlett's   72, 75, 76
Butcher's shop, Thomas Knighton   52-53; Alfred J Mew   58-9

C

Cabaret Kittens, pier entertainers   26
Cannon Cinema   57
Cannon Group, cinema operators   57
Car Park, Royal Spa site converted to   7
Casino Folies, pier entertainers   26
Casino, The, name of new pier pavilion   26, 31
Chad's Rock, Blackgang   78
Chalybeate water, springs   4, 17
Charles I, King   44
Cherbourg, fare Shanklin to   26
Chine, The   4, 6, 8, 9, 16, 24, 36, 43, 69, 78-83, IBC; its stone bridge   82; PLUTO pumping station   26
Chine Hill   6, 9; 'right to use'   6
Chine Inn   35, 42
Chine Road   79
Church, United Reformed, its tower   49, 54, 66; St Saviour's IFC, 28, 29, 43, 67, 91; Roman Catholic Sacred Heart   66; St Blasius   5, 70; lychgate with striking clock   70
Cinema, Shanklin's first   25; Playhouse   57; Regal   57
Clapham & Dwyer, pier entertainers prosecuted   26
Cliff View, Luccombe house   72
Clock golf, game played at Hollier's   63
Clock, Jubilee, Queen Victoria's   28; why on waterfront   15, 41; granted Listed Building status   41
Clock, lychgate with striking   5, 70
Coastguard Station   6; local lookout   6
Colenutt, William, invited to build Chine pathway   78
Cottage Hospitals   91
Cotton, Billy, dance band pier entertainers   26
Country Life magazine   36
Cowes, Somerton aerodrome   84
Crab Inn, The   44-48, 62, 78
Crighton, Connie, pier show entertainer   25
Crone, Thomas, furnishings and upholstery   55
Crossley gas engine, Lift augmentor   37
Croydon Aerodrome   84
Culver Cliff, Sandown   32
Customs & Excise station   9

D

Daish, John, hotel proprietor   42; director of new Pier company   25
Daish's Hotel   3, 5, 16, 18, 42, 63, 64, 65
Dancing over the Sea, Pier entertainment   26, 27, 34
Darwin, Charles, biologist   4, 6, 16
Dash, John, hotelier who changed his name to Daish   42, 64, 65
Deckchairs   14
Deek, William Thomas, chemist's shop   50
Devonshire Villas   16
Dexion slotted angle, lampposts made of   21, 26
Diamond Jubilee, Queen Victoria's   46; Clock   13, 40-41
Dodson bus body   85
Domesday Book   4
Drinking fountains on pavement   21
Dunkirk evacuation   84

E

Early Closing Day   42; introduction of   53; repeal of   53
Eastcliff Promenade   6, 36, 39, 43
Eden, Anthony, Prime Minister at pierhead attraction   26
Edinburgh and Connaught, Dukes of   16, 17
Effluent tank, Esplanade's sewage   7, 33
Eglantine Cottage   4
Electricity, Shanklin streets first illumination by   6
Elgar, Sir Edward   3; his marriage & Shanklin honeymoon   5
Enemy bombing attacks on Shanklin   44
Englefield, Sir Henry Charles, author quoted   16
English, Ernest 'Music is Fun' concerts   43
Esplanade Hotel   6, 16
Esplanade, The   3, 4, 6, 7, 8, 11, 32, 36, 42, 43, 75; *Illustrated London News* bombed seafront picture   92
Eton Lodge   6, 16, 22, 36
Everett, Edward, US Consul to London   68
Excise Officers based in Old Village   78

F

Farmers' Ice Cream   74
Fire engine, Shanklin Town   IFC
First World War   6, 7, 12, 16, 25
Fisherman's Cottage   6, 8, 9, 24, 35, 78
Flagpole at pier   7, 13, 19, 20, 25, 35; destroyed by Council   27
Fleming, Victor, conductor Midland Symphony Orchestra   43
Fletcher, Cyril, pier entertainer   26
Flotsam & Jetsam, pier entertainers   26
Formby, George, entertainer   12
Forster & Andrews, makers of pipe organ   70
Frederick of Germany, Empress   16, 17
French aristocracy attracted to Shanklin   3
Fyfe, Henry Hamilton, journalist quoted   42

G

Gas lamp standards   23
Gas works   29, 90
Gate-posts. cylindrical stone   17
Gault, variety of clay   5
Gazette, The, newspaper   5
Gem paddle steamer   24
German aristocracy attracted to Shanklin   3
Germany, Crown Prince of   16
Girls' Friendly Society   92
Glenelg   16
Godfrey, Fred (Llewellyn Williams), entertainer   12
Godshill, hydrangea nurseries at   43
Gold, Harry, dance band pier entertainers   26
Golden Jubilee, Queen Victoria's   40
Golf, clock, game played at Hollier's   63
Goods transportation before railway & pier   6
Govan shipyards, Scotland   1, 84
Grapevine, Royal Spa Hotel's   16
Gray, Harry, Rylstone House board residence   68
Great Storm of 1987 destroys Pier   27, 34; its damage   7, 34
Greek Consul to London, Michael Spartali   43, 68
Greenham & Co, wine merchants   53
Greenham, Alfred, mineral water maker   16, 17; mystery author solved   16
Grosvenor Gallery, London   68
Groynes, preserving sands by   11

H

Harrow Lodge   6, 16, 22, 36
Hatcher, Sid, taxi driver   16

Hatherton, Margaret, Lady 24
Heinrich of Prussia, Prince 16
Hellyer, Thomas, architect 91
Henry III, King 22
Henry of Battenberg, Princess 92
Hi-Da-Way Tearooms at Luccombe 74, 75
High Sheriff of the Isle of Wight (2002-3) 78
High Street, Shanklin 49-53; bus in 85
Highbury Barn, London venue 16
Hill, Eric and his Musicians, dance band pier entertainers 26
Hilton, Jack, dance band pier entertainers 26
Hinton, Archibald 16, 17, 42; director of new Pier company 25
Hinton, Charlotte Ann 16
Hinton's Royal Spa Hotel 16, 17, 19, 43 (*see also* The Royal Spa Hotel)
Holden Brothers, High Street motor engineers 60
Holland, introduction pineapple from 22
Hollier, William and Alice, of Niton 61
Hollier's Hotel 3, 4, 5, 16, 18, 42, 44, 61, 62, 63, 64; clock golf at 63
Holling, William, town councillor 43
Home of Rest 91, 92
Honeymoon Cottage, Chine 78
Hope Hill 9, 12, 16; Road 43
Horse-drawn bus *The Rocket* 89
Horse-racing at Ashey 42
Howe, 'Professor', pier entertainer 26
Howitt, Samuel, artist 78
Hydrangeas on clifftop 22, 23; history of 43-44

I

Illustrated London News view of bombed Esplanade 92
International Exhibition 1862 IFC
Isle of Wight Chronicle & Guardian newspaper 5
Isle of Wight Chronicle, Sandown newspaper 5
Isle of Wight Express Motor Syndicate 85
Isle of Wight Guardian newspaper 5, 60
Isle of Wight Infirmary & County Hospital 40
Isle of Wight Minstrels, pier entertainers 26
Isle of Wight Observer quoted 40
Isle of Wight Steam Packet Co 25
Isle of Wight Subscription Concerts Society 43
Ives, H A, Ventnor photographer 80, 82
Ivy-covered walls 61, 62

J

Jeffrey, Lord 5
Joachim, Prince, at Shanklin 16
Jubilee Clock, Queen Victoria's 3, 11, 13, 35, 40-41, 43

K

Kaiser, the, his younger son at Shanklin 16
Keats Green 22, 28, 31, 36, 38, 43, 67
Keats Inn 20, 23, 28, 43
Keats, John, poet 3, 4, 5, 42, 78
Kershaw & Co Ltd, publishers 8
King Charles I, Shanklin connections 44
King Stephen 5, 70
Knighton, Thomas, butcher's shop 52-53

L

Lake village 6
Lale, Edward, Shanklin boatman 10
Lamposts made of Dexion 21
Landguard Road IFC, 29; Manor Road gas works 90; Cottage Hospital 91
Landslip, The, southern Island feature also known as The Undercliffe 71, 72
Lavender, Harry, Lift operator 37
Leach, Jimmy, and his Organolians, pier entertainers 27

Lee, Sandown-Shanklin Aerodrome 84
Lemare, Edwin Henry, Ventnor organist 40
Lewis, name of undercover police officer 26
Library, Shanklin 46
Lifeboat Station 8
Lift, Newnes' Hydraulic 3, 6, 11, 22, 28, 29, 35, 36-39; how operated 36; demolished 37; Company's records 37; modern replacement gives cause for concern 37
Liggers, thatching feature 47
Lincoln House, Esplanade cottage 6
Lloyd Loom furnishings 16
Longfellow, Henry Wadsworth, poet 4, 5, 42
Lord Alverstone 91
Lord Chief Justice 91
Lord Mayor of Shanklin, Francis White Popham 5, 70, 78
Lorna Doone paddle steamer 28, 84
Luccombe Road 91; Village 72-77; Chine 72, 73, 74, 75; Common 72, 76; post-war destructive slips 75-77
Luftwaffe's aerial observation aircraft 17
Lynton/Lynmouth Cliff Railway 36
Lychgate with striking clock 5
Lyon's Tea advert 59

M

Macpherson, Anne (Springman) 24
Mais, Stuart Petre Brodie, author quoted 5
Mall, The 50, 53, 56, 59
Manor House, Shanklin's 24; Pond 71
Martin, Wavell Henry, bookseller 54
Martin, William Beavan, bookshop owner 52-53; introduces Early Closing Day 53
Martin's Library and bookshop 49, 52-54
Mears & Stainbank, bell-founders 91
Merryweather & Sons IFC
Mew, Alfred J, butcher's shop 58-9
Mew, Fred, author quoted 25
Midland Bank, High Street 53
Midland Symphony Orchestra 43
Milne, William Oswald, architect 43
Milnes-Daimler 20 hp bus 85
'Monopole', mystery author identified 16, 17
Moorman, C H 20; director of new Pier company 25
Morris Z pneumatic-tyred bus 87
Morris, William, artist 68
Mortimer, Charles, Steephill Castle owner 42
Moskowa, Prince de 5
Mount, Peggy, pier entertainer 27
'Music is Fun' concerts, Ernest English's 43
Musical instrument dealer 52-53

N

Napier Hotel, destroyed in bombing 7
Napier Refreshment Rooms 15
Napoleon I, Emperor 5
Nash, John, architect 40
National Health Service marks end for cottage hospitals 91
National Piers Society, president Fred Sage 27
National Provincial Bank 54
National Telephone Company office at Lift 36
New Forest, the 5
New Zealand, Summerhayes emigrates to 16
New, Napoleon Joseph, French soldier 5
Newnes, George, publisher and philanthropist 36; offers to finance Lift 36; his Hydraulic Lift 3, 6, 11,22, 28, 29, 35, 36-39,
Newport 6, 43; Victoria's Golden Jubilee Clock 40, 41
Newsagent, Samson in Old Village 48

Newspapers, Shanklin's 5
Nicholls Portrait Centre 56
Nicholson, W, Ventnor photo publisher IBC
Nigh family of postcard-makers 2
Nigh, Terry, family postcard archivist 2
Niton, landslip 71
Norfolk House, Esplanade cottage 4, 6, 16, IBC
Norman, Desmond, company director 2
Nudist colony, Southview Sun Club 72

O

Oatley, George, Lift operator 37
Old Village IFC, 3, 4, 44-48, 61, 64, 69, 74, 79, 83, 87
Organ, notable church 70
Osborne & Sons, gentleman's outfitters 88
Osborne House, Queen Victoria's residence 3, 16, 42
Osborne House, Shanklin Esplanade cottage, later hotel 6; occupants object to clock striking 40
Osborne Steps IFC, 10, 20, 28, 38, IBC

P

Paddle steamer *Southsea* 1, *Lorna Doone* 28, 84; *Whippingham* 84; *Gem* 24
Paint, pier, law suit regarding failure of 27
Palm Court, Royal Spa Hotel's 17, 18
Palmerstone Road 57
Pavilion, pier's first 7, 25, 29, 30; fire destroys 25, 30; new pavilion 7 casino built 26, 31, 32
Pavlova, , pier entertainer 26
Payne, Jack, dance band pier entertainers 26
Philip, Prince, and Queen Elizabeth ride in new Lift 37
Photo Precision Ltd, postcard makers 23
Photographic views, stereoscopic 45
Photographs, tintype style 24
Pier IFC, 3, 6, 11, 13, 19, 20, 25-34, 72; Construction Bill before Parliament 25; removal of steamer jetties 25, 31, 41; rebuilding of steamer jetties 31; steelwork from first pier pavilion used to build first cinema 57; Theatre 7; bridging wartime gap for PLUTO 32; post-war restitution 26; granted Listed Building status 27; Pavilion and Casino 7, 31; destroyed in 1987 Great Storm 7, 27, 34
Pierhead landing stages reinstated 26
Piers, Royal Engineers disable all 26
Pike, Mrs E F D, photographer 24
Pinder, Henry Powis, entertainer and impresario 7, 11, 25; his Sunshine Theatre 7, 12
Pineapple, form of decoration for gate posts 22
Pittis, Francis, house on East Cliff 43
Playhouse (Shanklin) Ltd 57
Playhouse cinema 25, 57
PLUTO (Pipe Line Under The Ocean) 7, 17, 26, 32, 33, 78, 92
Poltergeist activity, Honeymoon Cottage 78
Pomona Road 4
Popham Road 68
Popham White, Margaret 24
Popham-Macpherson, Mary 24
Population of Shanklin through history 42
Portsmouth-Ryde ferry 84
Post Office 48; on Esplanade 15
Poulton, Sir Edward Bagnall, animal biologist 68
Powell, Barney, pier entertainer 26, 27
Preventive Officer, his cottage 6
Preventive Station 8
Prince of Wales in Shanklin 87
Prospect Road 85
Prouten family, Chine Inn operators 42
Provincial Bank, High Street 50, 60

Punch & Judy show, pier entertainment 26
Putting green 7

Q

Queen Elizabeth rides in new Esplanade Lift 37
Queen Victoria 3, 6, 16, 66; her death 17; her Diamond Jubilee clock 13, 40-41, 43; her Golden Jubilee 40, 46

R

Railway station 76, 90; Shanklin-Ventnor line 90; last train to Ventnor 90
Railway, balanced lift 36; causes of fires in crashes 88; first train from Shanklin to Ventnor 88; funicular 36
Rayner, Frank, longshoreman and writer 6
Rayner, Jeremiah, hotel builder 42, 64, 65
Red Funnel steamers 84
Regal Cinema 57, 59
Regent Street 5, 57, 59, 60, 66
Richards, John Morgan, author quoted 42; Steephill Castle owner 42
Road accident, traction engine in High Street 59
Roberts, Caroline Alice, pupil and wife of Elgar 5
Robeson, Paul, pier entertainer 26
Robinson, Cardew 'The Cad', pier entertainer 27
Rocket, The, horse-drawn bus 89
Rogers, Shaker, newspaper proprietor 5
Roman Catholic Church of the Sacred Heart 66
Rookley 6
Rose, Clarkson, pier entertainer 26, 27
Rossetti, Dante Gabrielle, artist 68
Rowlandson, Thomas, artist 78
Royal Coat of Arms 16
Royal Engineers 26, 32, 33; Marine Commando battalions 78
Royal Household at Osborne 87
Royal Naval Air Services' (RNAS) hangar becomes theatre 7, 12
Royal Pavilion, Brighton 42
Royal Spa Hotel 3, 6, 7, 10, 12, 15, 16-21, 25, 28, 32, 34, 35, 42, 43, 65, 87, 92; PLUTO pumping station 26
Ruskin, John, artist 68
Ryde 40, 42, 43; new pipe organ for Town Hall 40; Theatre Royal 26; railway line to Shanklin 42
Rylstone Chalet museum 68; Gardens 14, 69, 76
Rylstone House 43, 68, 69; Rylstone Manor Hotel 68, 69

S

Saddler, Old Village workshop 47
Sage, Fred, last owner of Pier 27
Sampson's Warm Baths 9
Samson, newsagent 48
Sandown 4; bay 72; beach 11; builds pier 25
Sandown-Shanklin Urban District Council 37; creation of 72
Sandrock Spring, Luccombe house 72
Saunders, George Gordon, newspaper proprietor 5
Schmitt, Eugene, proprietor of Hollier's 61
Scott, Sir Giles Gilbert, telephone box designer 56
Sea Terrace, original name of Esplanade 9
Second World War 6, 7
Sewage effluent tank, Esplanade's 7, 33
Shanklin & District History Society 2
Shanklin Aerodrome Apse Heath 3, 84; attracts more German visitors 42; Bay Pier Co formed 25; beach early photograph of 10, 18; preserving sands by groynes 11; Chess Club 43; Cycle Depot 56; District Council 43; Esplanade & Pier Co formed 25; Fire Station IFC; Gentlemen's Club 23, 28, 43; History Society 43; Hotel, guidebook lists Williams'/Hollier's as only 42; Institute 43; Lift Co 53; Old Church - see under St Blasius; Pier Co formed 25; Pier Co Ltd, new business formed 25; Pleasure Pier 1; sands, early engraving of 8; Theatre 43; Town 42-71; Town Hall 43; Town Band 68
Shanklin, derivation of name 4
Shanklin-Whiteley Bank road 6
Shelton, Anne, post-war pier entertainer 26
Ship wrecks, high number in past 23
Shops Act of 1911 53; repeal of Early Closing Day 53
Sibden Road 6, 66; renamed 6, 66
Silsbury, Martin, newspaper proprietor 5
Sisters of Mercy, convent 67
Skylarks singing 73, 75
Small Hope 6, 16, 36; Beach 4, 33
Smuggling, Shanklin in time of 6, 23, 78
Somerton, Cowes aerodrome 84
South Kensington exhibition IFC
Southern Railway 84
Southern Vectis name 5
Southsea town 29
Southsea paddle steamer 1
Southview Sun Club nudist colony 72
Spa Bars, post-war development 17, 21
Spartali, Marie, artist 68; Michael, Greek government consul & hydrangea supplier 43, 68, 69
Springman (née Macpherson), Anne, owner of The Chine 24, 78
St Anthoney's Convent of Mercy 67
St Saviour's Church IFC, 28, 29, 43, 67, 91; pinnacle used as chimney 43; pinnacles removed 43
Stag Inn, Lake, The 6
Star Cinemas Associated Holdings Ltd 57
Steephill Castle, its owner 42
Steephill Road 56
Stephen, King 5, 70
Stereoscopic photographic views 45
Stillman, William J, US artist 68
Strand Magazine, The, George Newnes' publication 36
Summerhayes, his cylindrical gatepost columns 10, 36
Summerhayes, Willian Murley, developer 6, 7, 16, 17, 18, 20, 22
Sunday Entertainment Act prosecution 26
Sunday entertainment restrictions 26, 27
Sunshine Concert Parties 7
Sunshine Theatre 7, 12

T

Take me back to dear old Blighty, song 12
Tauber, Richard, pier entertainer 26
Taxi, Shanklin's first in speedy exit 16
Taylors Drug Co Ltd 59
Tearooms, Shanklin front 7
Telephone kiosks 56
Television, live show filmed on Pier 27
Temperance Seven, Isle of Wight Jazz group 27
Templemore 16
Tennis courts, Shanklin 7, 12
Terry Wood, Horace, pier proprietor 7, 25; builds a new pier pavilion 26; Sunday Entertainment Act prosecution 26; painting fiasco 27; Sadie, his wife 27
Terry's Bar pierhead attraction 26
Thatcher at work in Old Village 44
Theatre Royal, Ryde 26

Timeline 93
Tintype photographic process 24
Tit-Bits magazine, George Newnes' publication 36
Town Hall 7
Town, Shanklin 42-71
Traction engine in High Street accident 59
Trinder, Tommy, comedian 7, 26
Tucker, Sophie, pier entertainer 26
Twinkle, Clarkson Rose's pier entertainment 26
Twisted spars, thatcher's process 47

U

Undercliff, the (The Landslip) 72
United Reformed Church, its tower 49, 54, 66
United States Consul to London 68
Utterson, Edward Vernon, barrister and artist 43

V

Vaughan, Norman, pier entertainer 27
Venables, Revd Edmund, anti-pier protester 25
Ventnor, Environs of 6; railway station notice 89
Vernon Cottage 43
Victoria Avenue 6, 66, 85
Victoria, Queen 3, 6, 16, 66; her jubilee clock 13, 18, 29, 40-41; why placed on waterfront 15, 40
Victoria, Queen, Diamond Jubilee 6, 46, 66
Vine Cottage 47
Volk, Magnus, inventor 36

W

Walkden's Garage bus operator 87
Walker, A J, newsagent & novelty retailer 61
Walker, William, Rylstone House lessee 68
Wallis, Riddett & Co, estate agents 53
Ware, J Redding, author quoted 2
Watch House, Customs & Excise 78
Waterfall, Chine feature 78-83, IBC
Waters, Elsie and Doris, pier entertainers 26
Watts Gallery, Compton 68
Webster, Richard, Lord Chief Justice 91
Wheatstone, Charles, inventor of stereoscopic photography 45
White Popham, Francis, Lord Mayor of Shanklin 5, 24, 70, 78; Margaret, Lady Hatherton 24; objects to building pier 25; Mrs Margaret White Popham lays foundation stone for Queen Victoria's Jubilee Clock 40
White, John, local builder tenders for Jubilee Clock 40
White's Gazeteer for 1859 quoted 42
Whitechapel Bell Foundry 91
Whiteley Bank 6
Whites, Timothy, chemist 59; Timothy Whites Ltd 59; Timothy Whites & Taylor Ltd 59
Wiesbaden, comparison with 17
Wilkes, John, essayist 4
William the Conquerer 4
Williams, Llewellyn (Fred Godfrey), entertainer 12
Williams, Vaughan, composer 17
Williams, William, builder of first hotel 42, 61, 64, 65
Winchester House 92
Windust, June Brenda, historical observer 76
Winter Garden, Royal Spa Hotel's 16, 17
Winter, C W Ronald, author quoted 4
Woolworth & Co. Ltd, F W, shop 5, 60
Workers' Travel Association (WTA) 24
Worsley, Sir Richard, map of Luccombe 72
Worthing 67
Wroxall 72, 90

XYZ

YMCA Winchester House 92